THE LIFE OF A RUNNING MAN
A life of running from God

By: Robin T. Brown

The Reading Glass
BOOKS

The Reading Glass Books
(888) 420-3050
www.readingglassbooks.com
fulfillment@readingglassbooks.com

Table of Contents

Acknowledgements

The Life of a Running Man was inspired by my family, and lifetime of me running from God. If it had not been for the grace of God and His plan for me, I do not think I would be here. It took me going to prison for me to truly become a born-again child of God.

I would like to give thanks to my mother and father, Betty Jean and Lonnie Brown, for raising me with fundamental morals of life; my brother and sister who helped shape me into the man I have become; and Jud Wilhite, pastor and author of Central Church, for his encouragement for pursuing my dream. To the ministry of God Behind Bars through Central Church.

And many thanks to my beautiful wife, Gail; my two sons, Robin Jr. and John Wayne; and my brother, Larry Brown, "Pastor Grizz," for always believing in me and loving me unconditionally.

Also, to IUniverse Publishing, and to Samantha Lecky for her much- needed help putting my story together. I couldn't have done it without their help.

To everyone above, thank you from the bottom of my heart.

Sincerely,
Robin Brown

Preface

This is a story of a fifty-four-year-old man that starts as a young boy from a large family in Georgia that grew up in a life of poverty, moving back and forth across the country at a young age with loving, caring parents.

Then, to a young man who fell in love with a beautiful blonde girl in California from a broken home who lived with her mother, younger brother, and sister in a tiny two-bedroom apartment in Hesperia, California.

Then, to a young father twenty years of age with two beautiful boys born sixteen years apart, whom he tried to raise to be good young men.

Then, having gotten caught up chasing jobs and drugs.

To a broken man facing two to five years in a Nevada state prison — but, he received God into his heart; and this changed his life for the better and forever.

Chapter 1

My name is Robin Brown; and this is the story of my life. I was born to a loving, caring family in Georgia. I've lived a long life with nothing but love for them. We've had good times, and bad times; but mostly, they were good. It was a very large family. I had many brothers and sisters. Four of them were older than I was, and three more came along later. Can you believe I was the middle child of ten kids?

We were a bunch of rowdy kids too. We went on a lot of adventures together. Some of my earliest memories involve me playing with my brothers, and getting in trouble. My oldest brothers, Don and Larry, would go hunting for bottle caps, and then go on an adventure together. For those who don't know, you could take the caps for recycling and get money for them. One day in 1964, when I was about four years old, they took me with them and spent the money on a movie. The problem was, they never told my mom they were taking me with. Needless to say, she wasn't happy when we got home. She was standing in the doorway holding the switch.

A few days later, they were at it again. One of them was going through the shed, and found an old rubber inner-tube. They were playing with it a while before it broke. They tried to think of some way to use it; and that's when I came along dressed in my overalls. Don and Larry grabbed me by the straps, threw one end up over a branch, tied the ends to my overall straps, and kind-of bounced me around a bit. Then, they got an evil grin on their faces, and grabbed me by the ankles, and pulled me back as far as the tube would stretch and let me go. My mother was in the kitchen washing dishes, glancing out the window just in time to see me flying through the air buck naked. They had succeeded in shooting me right out of my pants. Needless to say, they got the switch again.

Time went by, we played, and tormented each other as kids do. Well, one rainy day, they were bored from sitting in the house; and they decided it was time for payback. So, Don, Larry, Joanne, and Dianne, my wonderful loving and caring brother and sisters, decided that they would try and send me away to some far away land by putting me in a suitcase and taking me out to the bus stop. I thought it was fun 'til I heard the bus and someone picked up the suitcase with me in it. Thankfully, it was just my mother taking me back in the house; she really did love me. Needless to say, they got the switch again.

A few years went by, and we moved to Columbus, Georgia. I had three more siblings under me: Rhonda,

David, and my baby brother, Mark. Now, I could join the ranks with Don, Larry, Joanne, and Dianne.

My dad was always working, trying to feed his hungry herd of children. Times were hard as they always seemed to be, but we had each other. I remember one Christmas in particular. Again, times were hard; but we had food. God always seemed to provide food. But I remember all I got that year was a pack of underwear and a blue a race car. It wasn't so bad because my brothers and sisters got a little something; and so we had toys to play with, and we always had each other. We were inventive and resourceful.

Larry and I used to take sheets and make costumes of the Lone Ranger and Tonto, or Batman and Robin. Of course, I was always Tonto or Robin, imagine that. One day, we were Batman and Robin by our old shed in the backyard; and we found some old pads and a mattress. We were taking turns jumping from the shed to the pad; it was a blast. Then, I had an idea – Batman and Robin took Joker, David, the prisoner up on the shed, and tried to make him jump; but he was afraid. He was only four years old; but he was the Joker, so we pushed him off. He bounced one time, and hit the ground. We thought we killed him.

In 1967, I was seven years old and my dad bought a '50 Cadillac; we headed to California. Just imagine, Mom, Dad, seven kids, and two babies, , with everything we owned, in a 4-door Cadillac, doing 55 mph driving across country. We slept at roadside parks, and ate from the grocery stores. We couldn't afford restaurants or hotels. I remember one night, I think it was in New Mexico or Arizona, my dad was exhausted, red-eyed, and frustrated from a long trip with a bunch of whining kids. He pulled into a Red Roof Inn so we could get a shower, and a decent night sleep. He pulled up to the office and went inside to get a room. The manager turned him away. The manager told him, "You have too many kids. I don't want my room destroyed." My dad was about to explode; so it was another night at a roadside park, washing up at a gas station, and eating snack food.

A day or two later, we finally made it to my Uncle Grady's house in Arcadia, California. It was a very long and exhausting trip for all of us. My dad started looking for work immediately. He found a few painting jobs, and rented us a house in Monrovia, the next town over. It was a pretty nice house; I think it was probably the nicest one we ever lived in. My siblings and I started school; and dad was getting a lot of work. Things were good for once. I think we had some of our best years there; certainly some of the best Christmases were there. My grandparents came out one year, and we had a great time.

I think it was the next year my dad bought a brown '65 GMC pickup with a teardrop camper. My dad took us camping up to the high desert, to a place called 'Hercules Finger' in Lucerne Valley. We camped one night in a dry lake bed. It was strange because when we woke up one morning, we could see a trail from where the rocks had moved overnight; but the truck did not. That was something that had puzzled us all; but it was the coolest thing we had ever seen.

The next day, my dad drove us out a long, straight dirt road toward a rocky mountain. We found a place to camp; and my brothers started exploring. We followed a dirt road to the top of the hill where we could see the next valley. It looked like another world of vast, empty desert –untouched by man.

We felt like real explorers. We hiked through the rock for a while, then finally made it back to the camper where my dad had a couple of kites. It was a blast for a while. That is, until a string broke, and we lost one of them. Being the determined kids that we were, we took the string, tied it to the other kite, and sent it up so high we could hardly see it. That was fun for a bit. Then, another great idea. We tied the other end of the kite to our dog, a little brown dachshund named '*Chiquita.*' A gust of wind came; and up and away Chiquita went. Picture a bunch of frantic kids chasing their dog tied to a kite out in the middle of the desert. I can only imagine what was going through Chiquita's mind. She must have felt like I did when Don and Larry shot me from my overalls, terrified; but we did catch her.

As the sun was going down in the beautiful desert, Don and Larry started a campfire where we could sit around, tell stories, and feel like real pioneers. This gave Mom and Dad some much-needed time alone together. It was something we had never experienced before: kids sitting around a campfire, telling stories, and listening to coyotes howl in the night. Larry, about fourteen or fifteen years old, was dressed like a cowboy with a .22 rifle across his arm. He was walking around the fire as Don was telling stories; and the coyotes howled. Then, everything got chillingly quiet. Larry stopped walking. A serious look came over his face. He started to squat down, and ended up sitting right on a yucca cactus. He sprang up with a blood-curdling scream. Mom and dad came flying from the camper, thinking Larry had shot himself.

He was bleeding like a stuck pig; and the rest of us were rolling in the dirt, laughing so hard that it hurt. Mom took him inside, and cleaned him up. We finally fell asleep; some of us still chuckling in the night at Mr. Cowboy.

The next morning, we woke up, ate breakfast, and started exploring some more. We did find something about two hundred yards from our camp; we thought this was the cause for the coyote's sudden silence the night before. It was cougar tracks, big ones, about 5 to 6 inches in diameter. That scared us all; but it was also exciting, something we had never seen. It shortened our camping at that site.

About two years later, we moved up to the High Desert where we had been camping before, to a small town called '*Apple Valley*.' Why it was called that, I'm not sure. It was desert; and only one apple orchard across the highway from Roy Rogers' house, and the Roy Rogers Museum. We lived in a three-bedroom house, and started school. We were there for a year or so. Dad had his own ambulance service; and things were okay.

Then, we moved to Hesperia; it was a town closer to the mountains with pinion trees everywhere. By then, there were ten kids: Don, Larry, Joanne, Dianne, the twins, me, Rhonda, David, Mark, Susan, and the newest, Jennifer.

Well, when I was about ten years old, things got tough again; and Dad decided to move us back to Georgia. We all thought, *'Not again;'* but we did. So, Mom and Dad loaded all of us kids, our dog Chiquita, and what little we owned into a car and a Plymouth station wagon, and hit the road. Don, about sixteen or seventeen at that time, drove the car; and dad the station wagon with most of us kids. Off we went; still stopping at roadside parks, eating snacks, and washing up at gas station— not being able to afford restaurants and hotels.

We drove into Tucumcari, New Mexico, around 7 AM. Dad and Don pulled into a grocery store parking lot with a 76 Gas Station on the corner. It was a little chilly outside. Mom and Dad went into the store to buy stuff for breakfast; while all of us kids used the restroom at the station. Mark and I were using the restroom when Mom and Dad came out of the store, loaded up the cars, and headed for a park at the end of the town to have breakfast. Meanwhile, Mark and I came out of the restroom; and they were gone. I was terrified, but Mark didn't really understand why. The only thing I could think of was to grab Mark by the hand, and run as fast as we could toward the park which was about a mile away. Terrified and crying, we ran as fast as we could through an unfamiliar town, in an unfamiliar state, in the middle of the desert. We finally reached the park where we found our family sitting around picnic tables eating breakfast. They didn't even realize we weren't there. I think that moment started my life of running.

Chapter 2

We finally made it back to Georgia— to a very small town called Preston, about 19 miles from Jimmy Carter's house. My mom and dad found a large, old plantation house out in the country with a magnificent old oak tree in the front yard. The house was white with a front porch, back porch, and side porch that faced the red dirt road that led from the house then went north. The house had five huge bedrooms, with a fireplace in every room; a dining room; and kitchen. We used the hall as a roller rink and boxing ring.

It had running water and indoor plumbing; but no hot water. The walls had no insulation, so it was extremely cold in winter. We would place bricks in the fire, wrap them in a towel, and then put them in bed with us to keep warm. We only had a few beds, so there were usually two or three kids per bed; and that helped stay warm.

Mom enrolled us in school called Ida S. Lawary Elementary School; she got a job as a teacher's aide there. There were only five white kids to the whole school; three which were my siblings. It was a very poverty-stricken area. Most of the black children didn't have shoes to wear; and most of the teachers were almost as ignorant as the kids.

My sixth grade history teacher gave us an assignment of places around the world, well, my report was on the Mojave Desert where I have lived for the past two years. When I stood up to give my report, the teacher stopped me right at the start. She told me it was pronounced as the Mo-Jave Desert, and gave me an "F" on my report. I took that "F" home to show Mom. I had never seen her so furious in my entire life. She went to school the next day; and let my teacher have it with both barrels of a double barrel shotgun. She turned that "F" report into an "A" report.

It was fun being in the country though. I got to spend time with my grandparents on my mother's side, the Walkers. I got to know my aunts and uncles. Uncle Frank, Uncle Thomas, Aunt Marie, Aunt Loreane, and all of my cousins came together to have huge family reunions on my Great-Uncle Noble's Farm. Except for the nasty gnats that swarmed in clouds, we used to watch Uncle Noble feed his hogs. He had the biggest hogs I have ever seen. Those were great days: going into Grandma's house, picking pecans from the orchard around her house, gathering veggies from her garden, shucking corn, snapping beans, and churning homemade ice cream.

Sadly, that was the last year we got to spend with Granddaddy Walker. He passed not long after. Now I think back, looking at him, he was an old American Indian man sitting in his wheelchair with the amputated leg from strokes. He was so doped up; I wonder if he knew what was really going on. Not being able to enjoy all of his grandchildren must have made him miserable. Thank God, he didn't have to suffer anymore.

Dad and Don got a job working at a mobile home plant in Richland, Georgia, a few miles from our house; but it didn't last. They heard about work in Mesa, Arizona; so they packed some clothes, and headed out west again— leaving Mom and the rest of us kids behind, while they hunted for work. They were gone for about two or three weeks before they were back with no luck.

We moved to Apple Valley again. We lived there in 1973 during my 7th grade year in junior high. We went to an Assembly of God Church in Victorville, where, for the first time, I accepted Christ into my life, and was baptized. Not really knowing the meaning of what I had done, I moved on.

So, from 1970 to 1977, we had moved from Georgia to California eight times. My best friends were in Columbus; and I had very few friends who were in California. My first best friend was Mark.

We looked after each other in the neighborhood. He got me my first job at KFC where I bought my first car, a '66 Bonneville from my boss, Bob, a tall Italian man with a nose the size of a banana. He was cool. Mark and I were sixteen years old; but Bob would leave us to close the store at night, trusting us with thousands of dollars, and no supervision. Well, that was until my dad decided we were moving to California, again.

So, California, here we come— for the fourth time. We stayed there one year, and then, it was back to Columbus. At the age of seventeen, I started working construction, and smoking pot. I began running with the wrong crowd and destroying people's property; starting the day I turned eighteen. I bought an ounce of pot, went to a friend's house, and started my life of being stoned; there I was, thinking I was cool.

Chapter 3

My brother Larry got married, and moved to California in a baby blue 1955 Chevy Bel-Aire. He joined a country gospel band. He is an amazing self-taught guitar player, and singer. He turned his life to God after he and Don were almost beaten to death in California a few years earlier. He is just an amazing musician.

His gospel group came to Georgia on tour on an old bus. They were there a few days; and the day before they left, God told me I needed to go with them because I was starting the wrong path. I didn't know it was God telling me that; but that is what I did. I asked Larry if I could go with them. He said that he would talk to Dale and Joan. They agreed. I told my mom and dad; they thought it would be a good thing for me to do. I struck out on my own at eighteen years old, just like Larry.

What I didn't realize was my life was going to be a life of running. I couldn't play instruments or sing; but I worked on the bus to pay my way. Lord knows it needed to be worked on. With Dale and Larry's guidance, we kept it going.

During the trip back, they stopped to sing and minister in places like Alexandria, Louisiana; Dallas, Texas; Houston, Texas; and El Paso. Then, to my favorite place, Tucumcari, New Mexico—where Mark and I got left at a 76-gas station as kids. Afterwards, we went onward to Apple Valley, California.

Larry let me stay with him, his wife Becky, and their two kids. Not long after, Larry and his wife got divorced; and she took the kids back to Georgia. That left Larry and I on our own. Right after my nineteenth birthday, Larry told me the group was going on tour again, and with some new band members. There was no room for me. That hurt me deeply; I felt abandoned, empty, and alone.

My brother Don lived in Hesperia with his wife and son; so I spent some time with them. Larry did let me stay at his house while he was gone; and their piano player left me his van to drive. A few days after they left on tour, I went to Don's house for dinner. We were up a little late talking of old times and things we have done. Don was also in construction, doing the same thing I did: running heavy equipment. He was working in Perris Valley, California. He had to get up early because he had a long drive in the morning; so I left and went home.

The next day, I woke up to an empty house. I ate some breakfast, and started out looking for a job. That day, I drove all over with no luck. When I got home, my sister-in-law called. She told me that

Don fell asleep at the wheel, and crashed his truck. My heart sank. He was alive, but he was paralyzed from the chest down. He broke his neck at the 7th vertebrae. I jumped in the car, and drove down to San Bernardino where he was in the hospital. I walked into his room, and saw him lying there all busted up. He was awake long enough for him to whisper to me that he loved me; then, he fell asleep. That broke my heart. I went home to an empty house, and broke down. Now, I had never felt so alone.

Chapter 4

Larry was on tour; Don was near death in the hospital; and I had no one to talk to but God. I really didn't know how to talk to him. Instead of trying, I got in the car and drove to Victorville to a shopping center, where my mom used to work, and everyone congregated on Friday and Saturday night. I parked the car, and got out to walk around a bit; but didn't see anyone I knew. I was standing on the sidewalk in front of the drug store where Dad used to take us for ice cream after church when we were kids. It was the only place where I felt any kind of comfort.

Then, out of nowhere, a friend of mine, Tim, drove up with two girls in the car. The girl in the back seat was a beautiful blonde with her hair feathered back, and a smile that would melt an ice cube. She looked at me, and told Tim, "I'm going to marry that guy." I hadn't even talked to her yet. Tim introduced us; her name was Gail Griewe, the most beautiful name I have ever heard.

We dated about six months. I met her mom, brother, and sister. It was a broken home. Her dad lived in Big Bear, California. He was a real estate agent. Her mom, an alcoholic on welfare, lived in a small 2-bedroom apartment in Hesperia. I spent more nights dragging her out of bars than I care to remember; but she was still a good woman. She was left alone with three kids, and didn't have God in her life. She had no direction. I did all I could for them.

We were at her house one night; it was cold outside. Her mom was in her room sick from being at the bar all night. Gail and I were lying on the floor, talking about our lives, when she started crying. I asked her why; and she said that her mom was moving to Hawaii. I asked her what was so bad about that. She answered with tear-filled eyes, "I have never felt so loved and cared for as I am with you, and I don't want to leave you."

Without hesitation, I told her, "I love you too, and I will never leave you." We both we both broke down in tears.

Her mom moved to Hawaii. Gale stayed with me, and we got married at a truck stop on Highway-395 just outside of Victorville on October 6, 1979. She was eighteen, and I was nineteen. We were two kids in love, ready to start a new life.

It was just a young man and woman from two different backgrounds falling in love. He was from a large, loving, and caring family that was always on the move. She was from a small, broken household. Both lived without God in the hearts.

Chapter 5

We were married at a young age; and went to Kauai, Hawaii for our honeymoon. It was so beautiful that we decided to stay. My wife's uncle showed me how to grow pot, and got me a job framing condos on the beach in a little town of Poipu. It was beautiful beyond my wildest dreams. We had a beautiful view of Mt. Wai'ale'ale, and a crystal-clear ocean.

On April 17, 1980, my first son was born, and we named him *'Robin Junior.'* Hawaii was an expensive state to live in; so my new family moved into an old, large house on a sugar plantation with Gail's grandma, mom, brother, and sister. This house had eight bedrooms, four bathrooms, a kitchen, a dining room, a pantry, and a large family room with a fireplace. The house was about three hundred yards off the highway. It had a long driveway lined with tall palm trees, a yard of grass, and a circular driveway at the house with a fountain in the middle. It was something you would see in a movie, absolutely beautiful. We were there about a year or so.

I thought I was in heaven. We had good pot to smoke, and plenty of cocaine to get us to work faster. That was a great job; but then, I took another job for more money. At my new job, I ran a backhoe digging swimming pools, grading tennis courts, and planting over 100 palm trees for the Poipu Kai Resort. It was truly a lifetime experience for a young man from Georgia.

In 1981, my brother Don, now paralyzed for the rest of his life, brought his son to Kauai for a visit. I've made some good friends who owed me a few favors. In return for helping work on an old '48 Trimaran and a Catamaran, Gail and I were allowed to set charters and run the resort boats. Doing all that allowed me to set up a charter for my brother and his son. I was so honored to be able to do that for him. We had a great time out on the crystal-clear Pacific Ocean, looking back onto the island. To see the look on Don's face as we floated out in that magnificent blue sea was absolutely priceless. I can picture that as if it happened yesterday. It was so great to be able to experience that with him; and I wish my whole family could have been there. Lord knows Don deserved it.

Don and Tony left a few days later. I hated watching them get on that plane because they were the only family I had seen in three years.

More time had passed, and the job I was on came to an end. Things were going so well at the time; but I was homesick for my own family on the mainland. I was spending all my time high on pot and coke; and I knew it was time to go home.

Gail and I sold what little we had; and with a couple of unemployment checks, we got on a plane and headed home. Gail's dad picked us up at LAX, and took us out for dinner because we weren't served anything but peanuts on our flight. After we ate, we went to his house in Hesperia where he had recently moved from Big Bear. We stayed with him and his wife, Jeanne, and their kids. My father-in-law bought me a beat-up, tan '68 Chevy station wagon, which was very generous of him.

A few weeks later, we moved in with my brother, Don, so we could help him around his house. Gail cleaned for days; and I got his yard in order because it was neglected for years. His wife left him years ago, and took his son. It was just him, alone in that house. His limited mobility didn't help him with cleaning; so we were proud to be able to do that for him. I was collecting unemployment checks from Hawaii; but couldn't find steady work. I was saving as much as I could. We were planning to move back to Georgia, to see my mom and dad where they had finally settled.

We were freaking out because we had some really important stuff in there, like the $900, a half ounce of weed, and some black beauties. We couldn't do anything but wait until it turned up—hoping someone found the purse, or we found it lying around. Thankfully, Gail's Dad called us after a couple days, asking if we lost a purple purse. That was Gail's purse! We ran up to go get it. Apparently, an elderly couple found it, looked through it, and found Don's business card. They told us they found the drugs; but decided not to call the police. At the time, this was a sign from God that said, "Stop! Let me help you!" But we did not listen, and we kept running.

In 1982, we wanted to move back to Georgia. We had a lot saved, almost exactly $900 cash from unemployment. We were going to exchange it for traveler's checks; and I asked Gail to get her purse. Unfortunately, she couldn't find it. That meant we had to backtrack to the house to get it, but we couldn't find it there either.

Chapter 6

It was 1983; and we were finally back in Columbus, Georgia. We started over again; working on construction, living in a camper, trying to get on our feet a little at a time. We were still smoking pot, and staying high. At the time, Rob, my son, was only three; and I was 23 years old.

One day, my younger brother, Mark, and I, the mechanics in the family, were replacing transmission seals in my dad's old Delta 88. We had finished the job; and I was removing the jack and the stands when it collapsed. The car came crashing down on my chest. Mark and David heard the noise; Gail and our friends came running as I was pinned underneath. It was a team effort to stop the car from rolling down the driveway with me pinned underneath. I was under the front right tire; and it was about to roll over my chest. Mark and David picked up the front of the five-thousand- pound car; my dad grabbed my feet to pull me out.

Dad drove me to the hospital since there was no time to wait for an ambulance. They admitted me with three cracked ribs and a collapsed right lung. I laid in the hospital for five days; and I thought, "Thank God my family was there." I healed pretty quickly, as most young men do; not really thinking much of how I almost died.

I went back to work a couple of weeks later, not giving a second thought to how God just saved my life. Gail and I rented a trailer from a man that lived down the road. We became friends, and started doing drugs together. I started driving a dump truck full time, running in Alabama, Georgia, and Florida. I was doing more drugs than I ever had, because, at the time, that's what truck drivers did. I was hauling asphalt up in Atlanta; and I stayed out of town for a few weeks, doing drugs with my coworkers. That is where I made the biggest mistake of my life.

I cheated on the one who loved me most.

It only lasted a couple of weeks; but I did it. I will never forget. I came home one weekend after it had been raining for a few days. Gail and I went to the auto parts store for a brake light bulb. I went inside for just a few minutes; and when I came out, I could see the look on Gail's face through the rain. It was a look of heartbreak, anger, and total disbelief. She found a note that the other girl wrote me, saying that she could not wait for me to leave my wife. I was so ashamed of myself; I felt like putting a bullet in my head. I could not believe that I had done that to the one person I loved and cherished the most. I had no idea I hurt her so much. She screamed at me, hit me with tears pouring down her face. All I could do was stand there and take it.

She didn't leave me; and I don't know why she didn't. I know in my heart that I made her, more than anyone else in her life, feel lonely, betrayed, and abandoned. I can only imagine what else she must have been feeling. I had never felt so humiliated and lesser of a man in my entire life. I truly wanted to die. I truly hated myself.

The years passed; somewhere in that time, she found it in her heart to forgive me. But still, instead of turning to God, I chose to run from him. I ran from the one who said he would always love me and help me.

In 1987, I had to get away from the trucks, my friends, and the drugs. We sold what we had, and moved back to Hesperia. I found work in construction again. I was making $16 per hour, the most money I had ever made in my life. I thought I had it made. We used the money, and rented a 3- bedroom house.

My sister-in-law, Terrie, came over from Hawaii with her boyfriend; and they stayed with us for a while. Terrie got a job. Gail stayed home, and took care of our son. I was moving up in the company, and didn't need Gail to work. I'd rather her stay home with our Rob. We bought a house in Hesperia. I was making good money; and things were better than ever. It was so good that I thought I could do more drugs; now, it was more pot and meth.

I was the most popular one around.

Chapter 7

It was 1989; and I was twenty-nine years old. I was doing drugs, but not nearly as much as you might expect. It seemed to be that way, at least. I was still doing drugs, smoking and growing pot, doing coke; and it had progressed to doing meth. I was now a foreman with the company. I had a company truck; and I bought a house, and a nice blue 1980 GMC truck with a white stripe down the side. I felt on top of the world.

We started a job in the middle of nowhere, in the desert, at the Fort Irwin Army base, Tank and Infantry, installing curbs, sidewalks, and gutters around the base. I was making prevailing wage, $28 per hour. That was the most money I made on a job up to that point; and I felt I was making it rich. My crew and I hid our drugs by the fuel tank on my truck to pass by the dogs at the gate. We thought we needed the dope. We were working sun-up to sun- down, on top of driving 190 miles a day round trip. I was exhausted. I did not see my house in the daylight for three months; and I only saw Rob on weekends because he was asleep when I left and asleep when I got home. The meth kept me alert so I could work during the week, and spend time with my son on the weekends.

Gail and I started arguing more and more. The long hours, not seeing each other except when I was dog-tired, and the constant use of meth and smoking pot so I could not sleep, and not serving God, was taking its toll on my family. Gail and I were on the verge of break up for the second time; and we'd only been married for ten years.

An old friend called me one afternoon, and asked me if I wanted to take some extra money; and of course, I said yes. He and his wife came over that night, and told Gail and I about a self- business opportunity. Gail and I looked at each other, knowing a little bit about it from Georgia; and we agreed that we'd give it a shot.

We purchased a startup kit, which was full of great products, a video, and some cassette tapes. We liked the products; we watched the video; and we listened to the tapes featuring guys named Al and Jimmy, who were successful in the business. Gail and I thought that was what we had been waiting for. We thought it was a good opportunity for us to start our own business based on what Al and Jimmy had said on the tapes. God worked in their lives, and changed them for the better.

We thought, '*This is what we need to help us out financially; and most of all, get us back into church so we could begin healing our almost broken marriage.*'

In 1990, we were off to a new start— going to church, going to functions, and surrounding our family with positive spiritual people. The only problem was that some of our directors were in the same boat with us; but the best part to this new beginning was I had never seen my wife more beautiful than in a dress ready for church or a work function. Things started off good. We had signed up a few people in the business; and it was off to a pretty good start. But we could not stop the drugs.

We would go to church only to come home and smoke a joint. Then, we would do a little meth. It did not take long before we were fighting before church, and fighting after church. Pretty soon, we stopped going to church and quit the business. The things we started to fix our marriage, we quit!

Chapter 8

We were back to where we started; except worse. We knew that we had quit what was best for our marriage, ourselves, and most of all, our ten- year-old son. All because of drugs. Now, I really felt like a failure to myself, my wife, and my son.

Later that year, the war in Iraq started. The man I voted for betrayed us. The economy crashed; and riots started in Los Angeles. Everything was falling apart. I went from $70,000 a year to less than $20,000 a year. I could barely keep a roof over our head. Not long after, I lost my job of six years. I lost my house. I lost my dignity. At least, I consoled myself, I still had the love of God and my family.

It was now 1993; Rob, now 13, was spending more time at friends' houses. We didn't even know who they were, or their parents. They fed him and gave him a place to sleep, which was more than I could do at the time. I just took it for granted that he was safe.

I sold my truck to my drug dealer because I owed him money. All I had for transportation was a 1985 Honda 750 I found through a friend as a mechanic at a 76 gas station. The house we lived in had no running water, no electricity, or gas. Our water came from the station where I worked, carried in whatever car was available to haul it. I heated our shower water in a solar shower bag, lit the house with lanterns, and cooked on the fireplace for almost a year.

A friend of mine moved to LA; he asked me if I could store his 1958 Chevy Apache pickup that had not run in 10 years. I said him yes; after all, my house was on two fenced acres.

In January, one of my old bosses said he had work for me in Mesquite, Nevada at $17 per hour. I said "Sure, where is Mesquite?"

He said, "About eighty miles the other side of Las Vegas on the Nevada, Arizona border."

I packed what little I could, and left Gail and my son at her dad's for a week. I got in my 85 Honda 750 custom, and headed out to Mesquite, Nevada. It was two hundred sixty miles of the coldest weather I've ever ridden in. I rode all afternoon and night, stopping wherever I could to warm up, eat, and get gas. It was, by far, the coldest I've ever been. I arrived in a Mesquite about 6 a.m., just in time to start work with no chance to rest or warm up; but just getting off that bike, I was fifty degrees warmer; thank God. If I had to spend another minute on that thing, they would have had to pry me off of it.

My boss was a tough but fair man. He knew my situation, and gave me a $200 advance, and a room at the Oasis Hotel and Casino for the week. It was another miracle from God. I worked all week running a dozer without a grade checker. A grade checker is a person who sets ribbons on stakes that lets me know how much to cut and fill the pads, and where the slopes and streets are, without me having to stop my machine to read the stakes set by the surveyors. So, on Friday, at the end of shift, I asked my boss if I could bring my wife the next week and teach her how to do that. I convinced him that it would make my job more efficient. On the plus side, it also meant another paycheck for me. He agreed.

I got in my Honda 750, dressed as warm as I could for another freezing two hundred sixty mile all-night trip back home. I arrived at around 12:30 a.m. after having to stop in Baker, California for a while to eat and warm up. It didn't help that I ran out of gas and had to walk, carrying all my stuff, the last five miles home. Gail was glad to see me much more than Rob; he had been spending more and more time with friends than home with me. We were really getting more distant; and he was only thirteen.

Gail and I left Sunday night, leaving Rob with Grandpa Griewe. It was a good opportunity for us to spend more time with each other; and a chance for me to teach her more about what I did. She caught on quickly; she was getting exercise; and I got to tell her what to do – that was a nice change of pace. We worked hard all week, and slept well at night; but we missed our son terribly.

Friday rolled around. It was cold and cloudy all day. At the end of the shift, our boss asked if we could work Saturday. As bad as we wanted to go home to see Rob, I told him that we would stay and work. The overtime money would have been great. Instead of heading home, we went back to our room, called Gail's dad, and told him we were staying another night. He assured us that Rob was fine, and for us to do what we needed to do. So, we took showers, got something to eat, and turned in for the night.

We got up Saturday morning around 6 a.m., got ready for work, drank a cup of coffee provided by the room, and walked outside; it was raining. It was a slow and steady winter rain; and of course, we couldn't work in that condition. Now, we got to go home to Rob; but we had no rain gear. I wasn't about to let a little rain stop us from seeing our son again. Being the improvising person that I was, I went to the hardware store, bought some black trash bags and some trusty duct tape. With those, I made us some rain suits. We looked like The Beverly Hillbillies strapped in plastic trash bags on a motorcycle. You could just imagine the looks we got.

Riding in the rain was miserable and dangerous; but we did it. We had to rewrap every time we stop for gas, food, or to warm up. It rained all 260 miles, except between Baker and Barstow where it snowed. Truth be told, riding in the snow was better than in the rain. We arrived at Gail's Dad in Victorville around 9 p.m. We were cold, wet, and hungry. Jeanne fed us some great Mexican food; and they let us stay for the night. This was very much appreciated because our house was still 10 miles away, with no electricity or heat.

We made this trip from January through the first week in March. Then, I received a call from another previous employer with a job available in Palm Springs. It was set to start the last week of March.

On March 15, Gail and I made one more trip to that cold desert town. When we had just gone through Las Vegas in morning rush-hour traffic, we said to each other, "We'll never live here." A shared chuckled passed between us. As we were going over the top of Apex Hill, at about 75 mph, I felt a vibration for a second; and suddenly, my motorcycle tried to go sideways. God certainly had his arms around us— I thought we were going down for sure.

I managed to pull to the side of the highway to stop. We got off the bike; and I started checking it to find the problem. I found that the chain was extremely tight; so I loosened it up, and proceeded to take off. As soon as I let the clutch out, it would tighten up. This went on for about an hour. I walked up and down the side of the road looking for anything I could use. No one would stop to help, not even Highway Patrol. So, finally, I loosened the chain to where I thought it would fall off. We managed to creep the last sixty- five miles to Mesquite.

We made it to the Oasis Hotel where we had been staying. I pulled it up on the center stand, and loosened the back wheel. All the bearings fell out on the ground. My heart sank. We were in a tiny town in the middle of the desert. I didn't know anyone or anywhere to get parts from. We were disgusted with the situation, and completely disappointed. We went to our room, took a shower, and then, went to get a bite to eat. The next morning, I got up and prayed to God to help me get a rear wheel, or some parts to repair it.

I thought I would go over to the job we had work done to see if my boss could help; but he was nowhere to be found. I had no idea what to do; and so I started the walk back to the hotel. As I was walking across the parking lot, I looked up and saw the company mechanic. He stopped to say hi. I told him about our situation. He told me that it was no problem, and that he was headed back to Hemet, California, where he was from, and had to travel right through Victorville. He told me to put the bike in the back of his truck, and he would take us home. Prayers answered. All I had to do was drive.

We got our stuff, and started back. As soon as we got on the highway, the mechanic fell fast asleep; and Gail and I smoked a joint. We made it right to our house in three and a half hours, the fastest we had ever made the trip. With our prayer answered, we took off at a sprint in full stride, running further away from God.

Chapter 9

Now with a new back wheel, I started my new job in Palm Springs, running a 633 scraper at $28 an hour. We were building the Palm Springs Municipal Golf Course. It was great: Gail was home with our son; I only had to drive 200 miles per day; and I was home every night. I still didn't have much time to spend with my son. He was skipping school, and spending more time with his friends.

My father-in-law was now part owner in an auto-pawn business. Gail and I went to see him one afternoon. As we pulled into the parking lot, there was a man leaving the office who was trying to pawn his '85 Yamaha 700 Maxim. I ended up buying it for $300. It had only 35,000 miles on it, which was a lot less than my 750.

The Palm Springs job ended; and I was unemployed again. I went back to the 76 station where my friend, Bob, still worked; and he gave me a job. He quit after a couple of weeks, leaving me to run the garage. I wasn't making much money.

In 1995, I got the notice that I had to move; but I only had two motorcycles to move with. Gail and I were sitting at the table; I was gazing out the back window, looking at this ugly broken down 1958 Apache pickup that was sitting on a trailer. I hadn't talked to the owner, my friend, in almost two years. Another idea popped into my head. I called Bob and asked him if he would tow it to the station for me so I could get it running. It was so ugly in a kind of primer red with a metallic green, along with about three or four other colors underneath. I started working on the engine; and Gail started sanding it. After almost a week, I had it running; and Gail was almost done sanding. It was drivable. I painted it primer grey with white spoke wheels. We started moving our stuff to my brother Larry's house.

About a week later, I was asked if I wanted to go back to Mesquite for another job. I thought it was another prayer answered. Now we had a place to go; and I could make more money. We could get the heck out of California; so off we went running again.

I ran the job in Mesquite, living at the Oasis Hotel during the week and going back to Larry's house on the weekends. It was summer time; so at Larry's, Rob would go to his friend's house, while Gail would sleep in the back of the truck under the beautiful stars. This went on for a couple of months. Then, Gail found out from her dad that her sister, Terrie, and her husband, Charles, lived in Utah. This was not far from Mesquite. We thought it was cool because we had never been to Utah.

So that weekend, instead of going to Larry's, we drove north to Terrie's— down a straight freeway of beauty. It was amazing driving through the Virgin River Gorge, up through the beautiful red rock mountains of St. George, passing the breathtaking Zion National Park, and into the high mountain and Green Pastures of Cedar City and Fillmore where they lived.

Chapter 10

We arrived on Friday afternoon. Charles and his grandma had an amazing meal prepared for us. We sat around talking all night; and we decided to go camping the next day in the mountains next to their house, at a place called Copley's Campground. We fished in the stream, and caught enough pan-size trout to feed us all. We stuffed ourselves with fish, and sat around the campfire, telling stories and playing with the kids. I saw my nephew swinging a stick at a tree branch; I asked him what he was doing. He told me that he was trying to get his ball down. I walked over and saw that it was a hornet's nest.

The next morning, that nest was full of hornets. Rob, now fifteen, fished some more. That was the most fun he and I had ever had together. We felt like how a father and son should feel. We needed ice to put the fish on; so Rob and I started to town. We left Gail, Terrie, Charles, and the kids at camp. It was the most time alone Rob and I had ever spent together.

Driving down the winding Mountain Road, enjoying the scenery, we came around a bend; and I saw a snake crossing the road. I have caught many snakes, both venomous and non-venomous, including the Mojave green rattlesnake, which was one of the most dangerous. I thought it was an opportunity to teach my son about one of God's most dangerous creatures. This was a five-foot long western diamondback rattlesnake. It was the biggest rattler I had ever caught. It was a beautiful snake with 10 rattles on its tail, and a button. I wanted this skin and meat. I guess that's the Indian in me. If I kill it, I will eat it in respect of the animal. So, I proceeded to cut off the head, explaining to my son how and why I did it this way. Rattlesnake meat— it was excellent. I cut off the head with a knife in my left hand; the tail was to my right, with Bob holding it down with the stick. I told him he could let it go; I fully expected the head to be severed. Well, it was not. The head was still attached by a small piece of skin on the bottom of its neck; and it bit me on my middle finger.

I could not believe that snake bit me. Instantly, I felt fire spreading through my hand, and with every heartbeat, it moved further at my arm. Rob was terrified. I told him to calm down; it was hard for him. I could see the fear in his eyes. He thought his dad was going to die. This was no joke; it was real. What started as a casual trip to town for ice was now a life-or-death situation; and no one knew but Rob and I. I took off my belt, and placed it around my bicep as a tourniquet. We jumped in the 58 Apache, and blazed down the mountain with Rob driving for his dad's life. We went through a few turns; and he slid front first into a ditch. Rob was frantic. He jumped out, bless his heart, and tried to push us out. I was praying to God to please get us out of this. As he did, I got behind the wheel, put the transmission in reverse, and backed right out. I told Rob that I'll drive, and he'll shift. We went down the mountain with God's hand on us the whole way.

I pulled into the emergency area at the hospital with my right arm swelling and on fire. The doctors took me in and gave me a shot of Demerol. Not long after that, I did not know if the snake bit me, or I bit the snake.

Meanwhile, Rob went back to the camp to get Gail and the others. When they arrived at the emergency room, I was out. She thought I was dead. About an hour or so later, I started to come around a bit. I found Gail frantic, along with Rob, Terrie, and Charles. The doctor informed me that they were trying to round up the Anti-Venom.

The doctor came back to me about an hour later; Gail and Rob were by my side. He said they had the Anti-Venom in Provo, Utah, about an hour away. About three hours after getting bitten, there was no available ambulance. The helicopter was also at least an hour and a half away. They gave me the option of waiting for the ambulance, or us driving to Provo. We decided not to wait. The doctor gave me another shot of Demerol, a pillow, and put my arm on ice. I got in the back of my truck with my pillow. Gail stayed at my side. Rob drove us to Provo as fast as he could.

I don't remember much of that trip; but we arrived at the emergency room in Provo where they quickly took me in, and started administering twelve vials of Anti-Venom. I was out for four days with Gail and Rob by my side. When I woke up, the nurse told me that if I had been fifteen minutes later, I would have died.

I thanked God for letting me live— and started running. I just would not listen to him. All he wanted was for me to stop long enough for him to help. My arm, still swollen black and blue, hurt so bad. Even the wind hurt. I had to keep it elevated, above my heart, with no support. This was hard to do. Rob did all the driving back to Fillmore, and then to Larry's house.

Chapter 11

We just found out that Gail was pregnant. We had nowhere to live. I had no job. And I just had my third near death experience. My brother, Larry, prayed with us. That night, I talked to my sister, Rhonda, in Alabama; and she said that she would send me $1,000 for us to go there. It was another prayer answered. So again, we sold what we had, loaded up the truck and a little trailer that Gail's dad bought for us, and headed back to Alabama to Mom's house.

We had a good trip. We took our time, and stopped to see the Grand Canyon Caverns outside of Kingsman, Arizona. It was awesome. Looking back, it kind of reminded me of the movie *The Grapes of Wrath*. Our primer gray 58 Apache with a mustard-colored Ford Courier trailer held everything we owned, on our way to a better life.

One night, we pulled into a small town in North Alabama around 11 p.m. to find a motel room. It was hard because everything was booked up; but we found one. It was raining; so we all took a shower, got something to eat, then laid back to rest after smoking a joint. We were watching the local news; and we found out there was a hurricane hitting the Gulf Coast. We fell asleep; and when we woke up, it was pouring rain. We still had one hundred miles to go. We ate some breakfast, filled up the truck with gas. It was then that we realized that we didn't have any windshield wipers. I had another idea. I took a piece of string, tied it to one wiper blade, ran the string through the window, out the other side, then tied it to the other wiper blade with a stick in the middle. I put Rain-X on the windshield. I had Gail sit in the middle seat, with the stick in the hand, as the wiper motor. Off we went, on our last one-hundred-mile leg of the trip.

We made it to Mom's house around 4 p.m. She had a feast prepared. It was so good to see them; it had been about eight years since I had seen my family, and there had not been a new baby in the family for a while. You know how grandma and aunties get when there's a pregnancy. I spent some much-needed time with my dad and brothers. We were getting settled in, staying with my sister, Rhonda, because she had a little more room to spare.

I immediately went back to work with my old boss. He had expanded his business with more construction work than trucking. He gave me a foreman's position where I could run equipment and a crew. Things got off to a good start. The pay scale in Georgia and Alabama was less than half of what I was used to in California; but I got a lot of hours.

Chapter 12

Things were off to a good start; but it wasn't very long before the drugs came back into play. Needless to say, we were back in the same old rut; and I was still running from God, the one who wanted to help me the most.

I kept playing the game, and not going to church. Mom and dad raised me religiously; and I was baptized when I was little. They would beg me to go; but my relationship with the church was ruined. I've met too many hypocrites to feel like I would ever become any more spiritual. I felt like I had love in my life, and children in my heart. I didn't need to grow my faith. I had my relationship with God in my heart; but I wasn't fooling anybody but myself.

February 9, 1996: I was thirty-six years old when my second son was born. We named him '*John Wayne*.' He was a beautiful baby; and we were proud to bring him home. Mom and dad were so happy to have a new grandson. I rented a trailer from a guy I worked with; it was one street over from Mom and Dad, the closest to them I had lived since I was seventeen. It was great. Gail and I could stroll John over anytime we wanted to see Grandma and Grandpa. They never really got the opportunity to see Rob grow up. They had not seen him since he was five years old. Now, Rob was almost sixteen years old.

Things went in a different direction, quickly. An old friend of mine from California called me from an airplane on his way to Columbus, just across from Chattahoochee River from Phoenix City, Alabama where I lived. He asked me if I wanted to help him and make some money. I said "Sure." Lord knows I needed it. That evening, he pulled up in a rental car, came inside, and we started discussing how we could make some quick cash.

He wanted me to help him because his girlfriend got busted getting off a plane in Atlanta with a quarter pound of meth; and he wanted to get her out of jail. I asked him how we were going to make that much quick cash; and he told me by cooking meth. I had never done that; but he said it was easy, and he also wanted to know if I could sell it. I told him that I couldn't sell it but knew someone who could. He told me what we needed and how easy it was to get the stuff. He had some cash; and so, we started getting the items. This did not take long. I asked where we were going to do it. My house was not an option because of my newborn son. He said that this was no problem; we would rent a hotel room with a kitchen. I will not go into detail, but it was easy.

We did that for a while. That is, until things started going south. I wasn't making any money. It went on for just a few more days. I knew it would be serious if we got caught. I'd lose everything, including my whole family.

Then, it finally happened. My friend Ken and my sister got busted.

The day she got busted, I went to work and came home for lunch. I found out later that his girl made the last sale to cops, and that she knew it. It was all set up. I felt so betrayed. I could not believe she would do that to us after all the years I had known her, especially with her knowing I had a new son at home. I was scared to death. I was afraid to go home; and I knew my friend was in jail thinking I knew all about it. I was as shocked as he was; but I did not dare go see him.

She was out the next day; and I confronted her. Of course, she denied it. She told me that she was set-up, which I knew was a lie. She had been lying all along. Come to find out, the cops were set up across the street, just three doors down, and could see everything going on at her house without having to go outside.

So, again, I begged God to get me out of this. I could not eat, sleep, or talk to any of my friends because I did not know who was involved. I expected the cops to bust down my door at any moment. I sent Gail, John, and Rob to Rhonda's house where they would be safe until I figured out what to do.

God answered my prayers again. I filed my income tax a few weeks earlier; and I got my tax check two weeks early. I cashed the check. I then sold my 58 Apache to my brother-in-law for $1,200. After, my dad and I went looking for a new vehicle. My mom and dad had no idea what was going on; and I was too ashamed to tell them. Dad and I found a yellow 1980 2-wheel drive Blazer that needed a little work. I took it home, put a new carburetor in, gave it a tune-up, and put two new tires on it.

Luckily, I never unpacked my Ford Courier trailer. I packed the Blazer, and told Mom and Dad that I had a better job in California. That broke their hearts. We had been there less than a year; and I was taking their new grandson away. I would rather lie and run than have them see me go to prison. I went to Rhonda's house, got Gail and the boys, stopped back by my mom's, and said goodbye. We started running again. I didn't say goodbye to anyone but Mom and Dad. Not even my brothers or sisters. No one. That was the hardest thing I had ever done. No goodbyes to the ones I loved.

Chapter 13

Our trip back to the West did not start well. Gail and I argued about everything; John was constantly crying; and Rob, trapped in the car, heard it all. I lied to Mom and Dad about the job in California because I did not want them to know about the drugs. But the trip got better as we went further away. Slowly, the tension eased.

We got to Flagstaff, Arizona, and got us a room. We again got a shower, something to eat, and went to bed. Gail and I discussed what we were going to do; this was different because I usually just told her what I was going to do. Come to think of it, that was what Dad always did. He told us what he was going to do. Man, how I felt like such a fool.

Instead of going to California, we had decided to go north from Flagstaff to see the Grand Canyon. This was a new adventure for all of us. Driving through Northern Arizona in the springtime was beautiful. The trees were blossoming; the grass was a perfect green; and beautiful flowers bloomed everywhere. We made it to the vast, magnificent Grand Canyon. It was unbelievable. Nothing we had ever seen could compare.

We stood on this overlook point, looking down through our feet into the canyon and the tiny Colorado

River. As far as you could see, all of God's beautiful colors blended with a cloud-dotted blue sky; and all we could do was stare. It was a sight everyone should see.

Gail and I said to each other, "Let's go to Terrie and Charles' house in Fillmore, Utah." At this point, no one knew where we were or where we were going because I didn't know if the Georgia law was after me or not.

We headed up highway-82A through Northern Arizona. We entered Southern Utah, another place of vast, beautiful desert landscape. It was truly a beautiful place. I am glad I got to experience that with my wife and sons. We drove, crossing the Glen Davis Dam just below Page, Arizona. Looking north, we could see the tree-topped mesas of Utah. We passed through a town called 'Hurricane.' What a name for a small town in the desert of Utah! But it was a beautiful place. We got on Interstate-15, and continued our last two- hundred-mile leg of our trip.

We arrived at Terrie's house late that afternoon, where again, Charles had a feast waiting. We ate, chatted, and went to sleep. I started looking for work, but with no luck. Not really much to look for in a small town.

It was 1997. After a while, tensions started running higher than ever before. There were too many people living in a small house. I talked to a friend of mine from California who lived in Las Vegas. He said there was work in Vegas. Rob was sixteen. I was thirty-six. We started out together for Vegas. This was the second time he and I got to spend time alone together.

We arrived in Las Vegas around 10 a.m.; and I realized that I didn't know where he lived. I did know what company he worked for; so we drove around looking for the company water tower. We finally found it. I drove on to the job site, and asked someone if they knew who we were looking for. Travis, my friend told me, "You mean the guy that drinks too much?" Rob and I looked at each other with a puzzled look on our faces; he didn't drink in California.

We drove around a bit, waiting for 3 p.m. to roll around. Then, I called him. His wife answered the phone. She told us that he was not home yet, but we were welcome to come over and wait. She gave us directions; and we went. We sat, talked, and drank coffee until he came home. Of course, he was drunk. I hate talking to drunk people.

His story had changed. Now, Rob was too young; and he didn't know where I could work. It was disheartening. Rob and I didn't want to be around a drunk; so we left Las Vegas, and went back to Fillmore. It was dark when we left.

It was quiet for a while as we were both disappointed. I was driving up Glendale Hill, I-15 between Las Vegas and Mesquite, when I heard a noise from the engine. I told Rob to turn off the radio so I could hear. It started as a tap, and then, evolved into a distinct knock. I thought, "What now?" I backed off the gas a little; and we made it across the mesa to where it dropped into Mesquite. It was knocking badly by then. I got up as much speed as I could from going down the hill. Suddenly, I heard a loud bang. It sounded like a shotgun blast. Sparks spewed from the exhaust pipe.

My heart sank; and I coasted about 10 miles, just far enough to see the lights of Mesquite. I remembered from a previous drive through Vegas that I saw a construction water tank. So, without hesitation, Rob hopped on his bicycle which we had in the back and rode five miles on a pitch-black highway to the Oasis River Hotel where my old boss was staying. Rob found his room, knocked on the door, and woke him up. I was sitting on top of the hill where I was all alone, looking at the lights of Mesquite, once more asking God for help. Lord knows I didn't deserve it. About an hour later, my old boss, along with Rob, showed up. He towed us to town, and got us a room. I called Gail and told her what happened. Then, we went to sleep.

As Rob and I were getting up the next morning, Gail called and said that she talked to her dad in Victorville. He had a truck without a title, but it ran; and we could have it if we came to get it. I thought again, "Thank God."

About three hours later, Gail and Terrie drove up to the hotel. We were on our way to Victorville to get a truck that Gail's dad gave us, and he also gave us $500. We stayed for a short time, then had to go. Rob and I drove the truck, while Gail and Terrie followed on our way to Mesquite. We arrived in Mesquite where we had a room for the night.

We got up the next morning, and said our goodbyes. Gail and Terry went home. Rob and I stayed so we could switch engines in the truck. We borrowed a backhoe to do the swap. We accomplished the swap in about seven hours. We got the Blazer running, and thanks my boss Dave for the help and the backhoe. He said to me, "Just get your stuff from Fillmore. Come back and go to work. They're starting a big job right behind the Oasis Hotel." Another prayer answered.

Rob and I drove back to Fillmore to get Gail, John, our stuff, and started running again. God was close behind, telling me, "Stop, I will help you." But I would not listen. I just did what I did best: run from God.

Chapter 14

I thought, *'The job came to an end about two years later. I have a place to go, and a decent-paying job waiting.'* We arrived back in Mesquite for the third or fourth time; I'm not sure since I had been around so much.

We had a room at the Oasis Hotel; and my job was directly behind it. Again, things were off to a good start. Work was going well. My boss, Dave, made me foreman after a couple of weeks. I never truly thanked God for what he had done for us, all I did was run.

One weekend, we would go to California to see our family, Larry, Dawn, and my father-in-law. The next weekend, we would go to Utah, to Terrie's. We stayed at the hotel for about six months; and then, I rented an apartment in town. Now, Mesquite was our home. I thought it was a good place to raise a family. I was making friends. An old friend from California was working with us. He would stay with us during the week, and bring us drugs to keep us up and alert at work.

It would be ninety-five degrees before the sun came up, and one hundred twenty degrees by 2 p.m. It was easy to get sleepy at work, which was dangerous, because we were running fifteen scrapers, four water pulls, five dozers, two blades; and I had to walk in the middle of all this while giving everyone direction. I had to stay extremely alert, or risk getting run over. For anyone who doesn't know what a scraper is, it's a machine that hauls about twenty-five yards of dirt. It has four tires over seven feet tall, is thirty feet long, and goes about 25 mph. It could drive right over a house; and then there's me, standing on the ground with all this commotion going on around me.

The job came to an end; and I was on unemployment. Things weren't so good anymore. During this time, my brother and his wife, Robin, a small Indian girl, came to live in Mesquite. Now I got to spend time with him. By now, he had been in a wheelchair since 1979. He and his wife had their own apartment in a complex next to ours.

Things got really bad. We got evicted from our apartment, and had to move in with Don and Robin. Gail had a job at a mini-market down the street, but didn't make much. It was barely enough for us to eat, and help out Don and Robin.

Chapter 15

By this time, Don and Robin moved to Oregon; and Rob's girlfriend's grandmother let us stay in their forty-foot motorhome at the Oasis RV Park. Dave had called with this job; but my truck was barely running, so I took a bus to Victorville where Roy lived. He let me stay with him. We were working on the same job, so I had transportation. I was there a few weeks, and was able to put a motor together for the Blazer.

Dave gave me a company truck to drive when Roy got sent to another job. One weekend, without permission, I went back to Mesquite and took the motor from the truck and installed it in the Blazer with Rob. I had it running again with its third engine.

The work continued; but now I was working in Orange County, California, which was about one hundred fifty miles further away from my family in Mesquite. The boss said that I could bring my family down; so, I took Gail and John with me while Rob stayed with his girlfriend in Mesquite. It didn't last. Hotels in Orange County cost four times what they do in Mesquite. John had an asthma, and didn't do well in the polluted air of Southern California.

One day, things got really bad. Gail took John to the store to get him some chocolate milk, his favorite.

Well, it turns out that the milk was bad. John was already doing poorly because of the horrible air in Southern California. Add the chocolate milk to that, and he had an attack. He ended up in the pediatrics hospital. We tried to get him out of the hospital so we could take him back to the desert where he could breathe; but the doctors would not let me. They tried to charge me with child endangerment. The next thing I knew, I was being held down by five orderlies. Gail eventually calmed me down; and I went to sleep in the room. The next morning, a new doctor went on duty. He discharged John, and let us go home. It was another prayer answered; and one that I didn't even ask for.

We made it back to Victorville; and John instantly started doing better. I had no job and no place to stay. Being the good people they were, Gail's dad let us stay with them for a while. Then, I got a call telling me things were booming in Las Vegas – and that they were looking for operators.

Chapter 16

It was October of 1997, just after our 17^e wedding anniversary, when we went to Vegas. I got a job running a Dozer with no cab. It was a job making good money. We were off to another new start. We stayed with my buddy for a few days; but we could not live with a drunk. Another friend, who we did not know very well, let us stay with him. It was just me, Gail, and John, who was a little over a year old. Rob was still in Mesquite with his girlfriend. I was working six days a week and doing well.

After a couple of weeks, I had enough money to get our own place. It was the first time in a year or two that I was able to do that for us. It was the first time in two years that we had our own place to stay. Lord knows we needed it. Rob was finally able to come home with us. Gail and I missed him so much. We had only seen him a few times in the past two years.

I was running two jobs as a foreman; and Rob was working with me. I was finally able to teach him how to do something after eighteen years. My boss came to me, and asked if I wanted to go to Reno to do a job for him. I told him yes. When I asked if I could take Rob with me, he agreed.

We went home and told Gail. She did not like the idea, but she agreed. Terrie and her family now lived in Vegas with us. She and John didn't have to be alone.

Rob and I were in Reno working sun-up to sun-down, making more money than we ever had; and we got to spend more time together than ever. We flew home on the weekends at company expense; it was great. We were there for about a month and only had two weeks left on the job, so we stayed without going home. With one week left, Rob and I got to drive my company truck back to Vegas so we could pick up some supplies for Reno. The job was almost done; but Rob wanted to stay in Vegas. So, I took Gail and John back with me, just to tie up a few loose ends. It was great. I got to show Gail some more of our beautiful country that she had never seen.

Two days before we were going to return to Vegas, Terrie called and said that Rob was in jail for possession of stolen property. Our hearts sank. I finished what I had to do; and we boarded a plane from Reno to Vegas. By the time we got home, Rob was out of jail at the age of nineteen, all from running with the wrong crowd.

His life of crime didn't start there though. He was always prone to trouble; and he hardly ever got caught. That kid was so good at running away from the police that every time his name came up on a police computer, I know those officers had to tie on some running-shoes. His arrest record started when he was fourteen years old. It was for driving without a license. Now, it was already a mile long.

It still made me sick knowing he had to experience something like that when I never had to. It was only by the grace of God that I wasn't caught; and I did come very close. It was around this time that he and I began to argue and fight more and more. He was getting deeper into drugs, and getting more out of control. He was off on his own path of running from God; and I had no one to blame but myself. I never tried to put him on the right path. I too had been running my whole life.

Chapter 17

Terrie and her family were living with us; and Rob had a couple of friends who stayed with us too. We were the closest thing they had to family at all. Our home life was stressful; but I could not turn anyone away. That's just how Gail and I were. There were people in our lives who never turned their backs on us; so we could not turn our backs on anyone either, whether we knew them or not. If we had an empty couch, there was always someone who needed to sleep on it. That's just how we were, and how we are.

That's how things were for the next seven years: never asking God for help when he was the only one who could help. I just ran, with Rob on my heels. We were both running from God.

In the year 2001, we were back in a weekly hotel one-bedroom; with me were Gail, John, Rob, and his girlfriend, Monica, sleeping on the living room floor. Not long after, our first granddaughter, Haley, was born. What a beautiful little baby. She was my little girl. I was so proud when she was a year-and-a-half-old. She would sit on my lap eating grapes and strawberries; she would love it when I put black olives on her little fingers and would eat them off. It was a beautiful sight.

It was really funny how she came to be; we had absolutely no idea that she was pregnant. Monica did a great job of keeping the pregnancy hidden from us; and it must have been a challenge since we were all living together. The day she went into labor was Thanksgiving. She left early – and we all freaked out. We were in Utah when Monica went into labor, Rob and Monica left early, by the time Gail and I got back to Vegas Haley was born.

Rob, Monica, and Haley lived with us in that small one-bedroom apartment on Boulder Highway; so we spent all of our time with her. About another year or so later, our second granddaughter, Breanna, was born. Except this time, things were very different. By this time, we were all doing drugs. It wasn't a lot, but we were still doing them. Monica's mother took Breanna straight from the hospital. She was just as beautiful as her sister was; but Gail and I barely got to see her.

I was on unemployment again; and the check could hardly take care of us. Rob and Monica did not work; and we all lived off of my $400 check. Not long after, Monica's mom took Haley too. Gail and I hated her for that. It was like taking our own little girl away; but we knew they had the money to take better care of the girls, and give them what they deserved. Monica's mother was a college professor, and her dad had his own office-cleaning business. We let the girls go without a fight; but it broke our hearts.

Now, it was just Gail, John, Rob, Monica, and I living together. We all started arguing; and Rob and I would get into literal fist fights. He and Monica would try to blame Gail and I for their girls getting taken away. He had no respect for us, or themselves. It was causing havoc in the house. John, who was in elementary school at this point, was trapped in the middle.

Chapter 18

A few years passed; and things did not get better. We were all running from God, and didn't realize it. I felt like a total failure because I knew in my heart that it was my responsibility to lead my family in the right direction; but I did nothing.

We were trapped in the small apartment; and Monica was pregnant with a boy in 2003. She did not keep the child. She and Rob immediately put him up for adoption without even discussing it with Gail and I. We despised them for this decision; and tensions got incredibly worse. We fought more. John was forced to watch; he had nowhere to go.

Another year went by. Rob and Monica were pregnant again with another son. He also went up for adoption without discussion. Things were worse than ever. The only good thing was that the two boys went to the same family, two professionals living in Reno.

Rob and I worked off and on while he was getting in trouble with the law. All I did was criticize them. Gail and I did not like Monica at all; but we still let them live with us. Monica's mother and father shunned her from their family. Without us, Rob and Monica would have nowhere to go.

Monica was pregnant with a third son in 2007. This time, they kept him and named him '*Gavin*.' He looked just like his dad. He was my first grandson that I got to see. Gail and I were as proud of him as we were of Haley and Breanna.

Things did not get any better. I worked off and on. Rob could not find work; so, he went heavily into crime, stealing what he could to survive. Rob was certainly on the wrong path, and he listened to nothing I said. Why would he? I was certainly not a good example for him or anyone else. I thought I was better than him and the people he ran with since I hadn't broken the law or got caught. This went on for two years; then, Rob and Monica left for Pennsylvania with Gavin to live with a friend. Gail and I were crushed; but we knew that it was for the best. If Rob didn't get out of Las Vegas, he would go to jail. Gail and I basically raised Gavin; it was like taking our own son away.

Chapter 19

Rob had to leave Vegas before he ended up in jail again; he, Monica, and Gavin took a bus to Pennsylvania in July of 2008 to live with his friend in Newcastle. Seven and a half months later, Rob called in tears telling me that family had talked Monica into leaving him and taking Gavin. I had never heard him so upset; and it broke my heart to hear him in such distress. He asked me for $300 so he could go after them. He found them living together in a rented house, along with a new boyfriend. I was very upset that Gavin was in the middle of all of it.

Rob made it there after a couple weeks; and he called me when he did. Gail asked to talk to Gavin, and then she said, "No… I don't want to talk to them. I want to see them." I still had some money from my income taxes; so Gail, John, and I used the money to go to Wisconsin. We missed them so much that we didn't hesitate.

We left at 5 a.m. to start our trip. The desert is beautiful at sunrise. We went through Mesquite just as the sun came across the Arizona Strip and into the Virgin River Gorge. The Arizona Strip is about forty miles down the I-15 that goes through the northwest corner of Arizona. The Virgin River Gorge is a section where a fault line pushed up the solid rock mountains into a vertical cliff, extending higher than five hundred feet off the edge of the freeway. The highway itself is mostly bridges atop the winding Virgin River. It's another one of God's creations that is absolutely beautiful.

When you get to the top of the gorge, the first thing you see is the beautiful red rock mountains and the magnificent Zion National Park, then you cross the Utah State Line into St. George, another beautiful city. I drove another thirty-nine miles to Cedar City. There, we got gas and ate breakfast at a café. We were all anxious to get on the road; so we did not waste any time.

I love the beauty of Southwest Utah. The tree filled mountains and the vast green meadows up through the small town of Beaver and onto the I-75 East through the mountains, into Selena, a small mining town. It was all new territory for us. We had never been further than Springfield. It turned back into a vast open desert, as far as you could see. This was one of the most beautiful deserts I have been through. It was a rainbow of colors, and had vertical cliffs extending hundreds of feet into the sky, ending at great plateaus that extended as far as you could see in any direction. Southeast Utah is just as beautiful and magnificent as the West.

It was around 1 p.m. when we crossed into Southwest Colorado and into the town of Grand Junction. It is also a beautiful place. In fact, if one has the opportunity, the entire Southwest is a must-see place.

Some of the most beautiful was yet to come. We started up the Rocky Mountains with the great Colorado River winding along the side of the highway up to Aspen. This was probably the most beautiful of the mountain cities I have ever been through. The river ran right through the middle of town, with condos and hotels on both sides. It was so beautiful that we had to stop. We decided to get gas and eat lunch, so we can take in the beauty of the great Rocky Mountains.

It was about three in the afternoon. We did not stay too long because we wanted to see the rest of the mountains in the daylight. It turned out to be a good decision. The top half of the Rockies was more beautiful than the bottom half. The river was even greater than in Aspen; and we drove through some amazing tunnels through the mountains at least a thousand feet long.

We made it to the top at the Continental Divide, where the Colorado River splits and runs south west and the Eagle River runs east. We stopped for a few minutes to take some pictures, then continued on to the mile-high city of Denver. It was rush hour. I continued through town, and drove all the way to the Nebraska State Line. About 20 miles in, we stopped and got a room at a motel. The motel gave me a senior discount even though I was only forty-six of the time; I must have looked like I needed some beauty sleep, and a lot of it. We took showers, and got a good night's sleep. We got up around 8 a.m., and went on our way.

We drove down the I-80 to a truck stop where I got gas and some breakfast. It was pretty good at a reasonable price. After we were finished, we continued the journey through Nebraska, a state of what look like oceans of wheat and corn fields, with giant windmills as far as you could see.

We stopped in Omaha for gas and lunch, and then drove on to Madison, Wisconsin where we stopped for the night. It was about 2 a.m., so we slept in the truck. I did not want to get a room for only a few hours. We were up before sunrise, so I drove through Madison to a small town for gas and some breakfast. At this point, there was only sixty miles to go before getting to Monica's house. It was overcast and foggy in places; but Wisconsin is a beautiful state full of pine trees and rolling farmland. Then, we found ourselves in Wisconsin Dells, a town filled to the brim with water parks, with restaurants built right in the middle of it all. It was pretty amazing. We didn't stop; we wanted to see Rob and Gavin.

We called Rob; and he met us at a shopping center. We followed him to Monica's house. It was so good to see them because it had almost been a year since we saw them last. That was the longest we had ever been away from Gavin; and he had gotten so big. There was grass in the front and back of the house, and a fire pit in the backyard. It was a really nice white house with three bedrooms and a huge basement. I brought Gavin a kid size fishing pole; and I took him to the backyard and taught him out a cast it. He did really good. Gavin really wanted to camp out; so we went and bought a small tent.

While we were shopping, he saw a remote-control quad with a rider that he had to have; so we got that too. I felt like spoiling him; no one was going to stop me. Spoiling kids is what Grandpas do. We went back to the house; and eight batteries later, Gavin played with the quad until dark. I started a fire in the pit. After, we told stories and talked about what had been going on. To be honest, Rob and Monica kept a lot of their problems secret from us and the rest of the family. We knew that they were having a rough patch, and that it was drug related; but we didn't know much else. John and Rob went in the house; and Gavin and I got in the tent. However, we didn't stay long. The mosquitoes were so bad that we went in the house to sleep.

Gavin wanted to go fishing in the morning after breakfast. Gail, John, and I took him to the Wisconsin River to fish for a while. We were gone about three or four hours when Rob and Monica drove up. Because we were gone for so long, they thought we took Gavin and headed home. I thought it was funny because it did cross my mind. After what Gavin had been through in the past few months, how could I not think it? Still, I could not do that because he loves his mom and dad very much. We were not catching anything; so we went back to the house.

We were at the house for a few hours when Monica's mom called and said that she was at the airport in Madison. Monica's grandfather had died; and she would be at the house in an hour. We needed to leave because she would have a fit if she knew that we were there with Rob; she does not like us, and especially hates Rob.

We left and got a room at the motel for the night. We were so upset because we only got to visit for three days, and now, we had to leave. Rob and Monica brought Gavin to our room. Monica left; but Rob and Gavin stayed for the night. Monica's mom was staying for two weeks; so we had to take Rob with us, and go home the next morning.

It was heartbreaking when Monica came back to get Gavin the next morning. We all cried as we said our goodbyes. They left; and we went to our truck to leave. It had rained overnight. Everything in the back was wet. All of us were crying for the first fifty miles. We didn't want to leave Gavin; but he wanted to stay with his mommy. We understood; but it did not make it any easier.

We went west to Dubuque, Iowa, where we crossed the mighty Mississippi River. Iowa came up out of the river, and into a tree-filled mountain. Now, I had crossed that Great River at the top and bottom. Ten miles in Iowa was oceans of cornfield waving in the breeze like the waves on the ocean? Then, we turned south down I-80, and onto the way home. This time, I timed it so the places we drove through in the day time, we now drove through at night. Rob helped me drive; so we drove continuously until we got back home.

A few months later, Rob and Monica sorted out their differences; and Monica and Gavin came back to live with us. We were all together again.

Chapter 20

I think it was late 2008 when Larry called and asked if Gail, Dons, and I wanted to go to Don's house in Oregon for Thanksgiving. Of course, I agreed. We hadn't seen Don and Robin in many years. We were excited. We packed our stuff, and drove down to Larry's house in Hesperia.

We arrived at Larry's house at about 1 p.m. on a Monday. We visited them for a couple of hours, and then, we went to Gail's dad's house in Victorville. It had been a long time since we had seen them; it was a good visit. Jeanie cooked us a great Mexican dinner. I think it was wet burritos and green sauce. She makes the best. It was the first time John had ever had them; and he loved it. We visited a short while, then drove back to Larry's where we slept for the night.

We got up early the next morning, took showers, and left for Don's. We stopped at a cafe on Main St. by the freeway I-15 for breakfast. We had a blast. We have fun anytime Larry and I go to a restaurant together. We had the whole family laughing, as we usually do, and were having fun with the waitresses. I had pancakes with two eggs, sunny side up with a side of bacon. I don't remember what everyone else had; all I remember was seeing two eggs looking at me atop three great pancakes. We blessed our food and got our fill, and prayed for a safe trip to Don's.

It was overcast and cool when we started on Highway-395 headed to Tehachapi. I called Mom and told her where we were headed. She was thrilled that we were going to Don's for Thanksgiving. She wished us a safe trip, then I lost my phone service. That was when I found out I did not have nationwide service.

We were having a good time driving. It was the first time John had seen a windmill farm. There were hundreds on the hillsides as far as you could see. He also got to see thousands of acres of farmland where a lot of our food comes from. There were ranges, almonds, walnuts, and even rice patties for miles.

We drove through Fresno through the San Joaquin Valley. It was getting dark when we went through Sacramento; but we continued on through Redding and up to Mount Shasta where Don used to live years ago. We stopped and got a bite to eat. I think it was raining lightly. It was also cold. We ate and stretched our legs a bit, then continued on. It was about 11 p.m. when we stopped in a little town to get a room for the night. We were all tired; and Larry, the old man that he was, needed his beauty sleep. Believe me, he needed a lot of that.

We got up early the next morning, ate breakfast, and continued on the last leg of our trip. We crossed into Oregon. Northern California and Oregon have the most beautiful mountains, scattered clouds, and a beautiful blue sky. We stopped at a little café in the mountains for lunch. It was a little pricey, but offered good food for a small town. After we ate, we decided to walk around through some of the shops. Most of them had Native American items. This caught our attention because we are part Indian, from the south. After we looked around, we got on our way. We only had about seventy miles to go before we got to Coos Bay, where Don lived.

We arrived around noon; and we were eager to see Don and Robin. Coos Bay is a beautiful place, with mountains on one side, and the wondrous Pacific Ocean on the other. That is the first time John had ever seen the ocean. What a great place to see it, on the northwest coast. The salty air was clean and fresh.

Robin met us at a grocery store, and led us to their house. It was a nice house on the reservation in a cul-de-sac. Robin's mother lived just two doors down. It was so good to see them; and we got to meet Robin's family as well. It was certainly a full house.

That evening, one of Don and Robin's friends brought over blue crabs that they had just caught and boiled. Everyone ate fresh crab. After they were all full, there were still three crabs left. No one else wanted any; so I had to eat the rest. Everyone laughed at me as I sat the table by myself, stuffing the crab down my face with juice running down my face and arms. I felt like a pig; but I was a happy pig. I thought I would have crab claws coming out of my ears. I had to walk sideways to get out from the table.

Then, Larry and I went out back to gather some wood so we could build a fire in the fire pit. We brought Don out in his wheelchair, and sat around the fire like we used to, telling stories. To see the smile on Don's face was priceless. You could tell that it meant a great deal to him to have us there, as well as Larry and I.

It started to drizzle. We were also running out of wood. We called it a night then, took Don in the house where we talked a while longer, and then went to bed. The house was full; so Larry and Dawn slept at Robin's mom's house, and Gail, John and I slept in the living room.

The next morning, Don was not feeling well so he stayed in bed a while longer. Robin took us to breakfast at a little café on the way to the grocery store to buy the fixing's for Mom's dressing, something that Don had not had in years. Gail has the recipe down pat. Gail and I argued over how to boil the onions and celery; but we were having a fun time doing it. We kept everyone laughing, having a good time. In the end, we did it her way; and the dressing turned out just like Mom's, perfect as always. The smell of it had Don out of bed before long.

Finally, the dressing, along with everything else, was done; now it was time to eat. Everyone gathered around Larry, and said Grace; and we all began to feast. And what a feast it was! Gail was so proud. Don and Larry said the dressing taste just like how it was when Mom made it; and it did taste like that, without a doubt. We all ate until we could eat no more. The only thing better than the food was being able to share it with my two brothers and our families. It was truly something to be thankful for. As usual, after dinner, most of us adults took a nap.

When we woke up, Larry, John, and I went down the street to an empty lot and gathered a little firewood, then we went back to Don's. Just before sunset, some new cousins and in-laws took us to an overlook where we watched the sunset over the beautiful Pacific Ocean. We listened to the ocean waves pounding on the shore. In the distance, we could hear the seals barking.

Eventually, we went back to John's. We built a fire in the pit out back again; and we all sat around the fire, telling stories and talking about our lives. We spent as much time with Don as we could, because we had to leave on Friday. As we sat around the fire, a cold front moved in; and it began to rain again. We had to retreat to the house where we talked some more before going to sleep.

We got up early Friday morning; and Robin made us breakfast. We took showers, and had to dreadfully say our goodbyes. I know it was especially hard for Don; but we had to go. Our visit was not, at all, long enough.

Larry, Dawn, Gail, John, and I decided we would take a different way home than the way we came. So, we took Highway-1 down the coast. It was one of the most beautiful trips we had ever taken: beautiful trees, the ocean's pounding waves, and ocean mist blowing off the rocks off shore, and scattered clouds in the sky. It looked like a postcard view, but it was a 360- degree real life view. We passed cranberry ponds, elk farms, and amazing harbors.

As we crossed over into California, the scenery got even more amazing. Now, there were some of God's greatest creations. The gigantic California redwood trees extended all the way to the cliffs on the shore.

We had to stop for a few minutes at a roadside park. We got out and walked up to these magnificent trees overlooking the ocean. If you have never seen one, these trees have a trunk about 8 to 12 ft. in diameter, are 100 to 200 ft. tall, and have bark so big it is hard to describe. John was truly amazed. I was so glad to be able to let him experience that, especially with us. People come from all around the world to see these trees.

We continued down the coast, passing through small fishing harbors with cottages scattered along the coast. I cannot say how blessed I felt having been able to make this trip with my brother and our families. We continued on to the town of Eureka, then to Highway-72; then, it was only eighty miles to Redding. However, it took us almost three hours. The highway twisted around the beautiful mountains of Northern California.

It started raining as we were driving through town and all the way to Fresno where we got a room for the night. We were all exhausted, and ready for a good night sleep. We got up early Saturday morning, ate breakfast next to the hotel, and continued on our last leg of the trip home. We stopped at a big farmer's market at the bottom of the Tehachapi Mountains. It wasn't really what we expected, but it was nice. We got to stretch our legs, which felt good; and then we started home. We went through the mountain pass, passed the windmill farm, and back to the desert.

When we got back, I called Mom and told her how great our trip was with Don, and how proud she would have been of Gail's dressing. Just to make her laugh, I told her how mean Larry was to me on the trip. I love to make Mom laugh, even if I have to tell stories about Larry. It's all in good fun.

It was overcast and cool when we got back to Larry's around 5 p.m. We stayed for a little while, then said our goodbyes. We thanked Larry and Dawn for inviting us to go with them. It was a trip that we will always remember and cherish.

After we left Larry's, we stopped by our friend's house. Then, we headed to Don and Jeanie's for a bit before we headed back home to Las Vegas. We finally arrived home around midnight. We were exhausted; and sleep came easy. What a great trip it was.

Chapter 21

In 2008, things were rough. We were living in Gail's sister's house in Fillmore, Utah for two or three months before the President implemented the stimulus check. When we left for Vegas to pay some bills, she didn't want us to come back. Thankfully, a friend let us stay in a tent in her backyard. It was miserable. It was summer time; and daytime temperatures were almost 118 degrees. Things literally melted in our tent. John's friend's mom let him sleep in the house; and Gail and I had a small swamp cooler that we could only run at night.

My unemployment ran out a few weeks prior; so things were really bad. I had heard on the news about an unemployment extension that had just been approved; so I called. I was approved. Three days later, I had $1,200 on my card. It was another prayer answered.

It was time to get out, and finally do something for ourselves. John was now twelve years old, so Gail and I took him for a ride in our 2001 white GMC Sierra. We started for Boulder City to see the Hoover Dam; and we ended up in Kingman, Arizona, at Gail's Uncle's House, whom we had not seen since 1983. We had a great visit that was only a couple hours long; then we started back for Vegas because John had school the next day.

I got a call from the union with a job in town on Blue Diamond Highway with a company that I had previously worked for. That was the best news I have had since my grandson, Gavin, was born. I started work; and after two weeks, the family moved into another weekly apartment. We finally had a good bed to sleep in, a cable TV to watch, and best of all, air conditioning.

I had been working for a few months; and my mom called me on my birthday, January 30th. She told me that my dad had another stroke, but he was doing okay. He still had his memory of his many children and grandkids.

After a week or so, I got my income tax return. I paid my bills and had enough left for a trip. I went to work and asked my boss if I could take a few days off to see my dad while he still had his memory. He told me to do what I needed to do.

I arranged three plane tickets for Gail, John, and myself to fly home to see Dad. I got the tickets at a good price. I also told Gail that I wanted to send Rob and Gavin a bus ticket to Mom's house from Pennsylvania. She thought it was a great idea. I told Mom we were coming. She was thrilled. However, I did not tell her Rob and Gavin were also coming; I thought it would be a nice surprise. She had not seen Rob since he was sixteen, and had never seen Gavin.

We arrived in Birmingham, Alabama. My brother, David, picked us up at the airport. It was about a one-hour trip. On the way, I told David about Rob and Gavin; but no one else.

We arrived at mom's house, where, as usual, she had a feast waiting for us. We ate and talked a bit. Rob called and said that he and Gavin would be arriving in about an hour at the Columbus Greyhound Station. Gail, David, and I picked them up. We left John at Grandma's house because we needed room in the truck. Plus, Grandma and Grandpa had not seen John since he was three months old; and he was now twelve years old.

David told Mom he was taking us to see a few new things in town to keep her suspicions low; then we returned with Gavin and Rob for a late Christmas gift. You could only imagine the look on Grandma and Grandpa's face. They were so happy. I think it was the best gift they had ever received; and it made Gail and I so happy and proud to be able to give it to them. I thought they would explode with joy. We had a great time; and we had barely seen any of them since David brought Mom and Dad to visit for a few days after Gavin was born and he had won $150,000 on a scratch-off lottery ticket. Our trip only lasted a few days; I had to get back to work. My sister,

Joanne, drove us to the airport in Birmingham. We said our goodbyes and flew home; but Rob and Gavin left to Pennsylvania.

We came back from our trip, and continued work. That job lasted about a year; and we did okay. But on a bad note, John wasn't going to school. I would be at work, and he would not get up to leave. He gave Gail such a hard time. I would come home from work, and Gail would be in tears. I tried everything to get him to go to school. I disciplined him, took things away, and even tried to pay him; but he would not go.

We moved into a fifth-wheel trailer with two rooms built in at another friend's house off of Lake Mead Boulevard. My friend, Larry, lived with his wife, Rose, his brother-in-law, and his mother-in-law. They all lived in a big two-story house; while Gail, John, and I lived in the trailer in their three- quarters of an acre backyard. It was private and cool; they were good people.

They let us stay there cheap. I was now on unemployment, again. My friend, Larry, and I were like brothers. We had worked together for years in the past, and had a lot in common. He had been in prison before; but he was a good man who just made some wrong decisions when he was younger. We all did.

It wasn't long after that Rob, Monica, and Gavin moved back to Vegas. They moved in with us. We were so glad to see them, especially Gavin. We missed him so much. Rob couldn't find work, well, none of us could. He went right back to the same old tricks. He went back to stealing things to survive.

Chapter 22

In 2009, Rob went to prison for a year. As sad as we were to know he was behind bars, we thought it was best for him. He caused us so much stress and grief that it was impossible living with him. His life of crime was put to a halt; so prison was the best place for him.

Monica and Gavin stayed with us for a while; then her mom let her and Gavin move back in. Gail and I thought that was great. Now, Gavin got to meet and live with his two older sisters. He was as happy as could be. He finally got to see his sisters.

We all started going fishing a lot. We had a great time. We would go out to Cold Creek up by Mount Charleston, different ponds and parks around town, and to Lake Mead where we did a lot of night fishing.

Rob had been moved to a Work Camp up in Pioche, Nevada. He wanted us to come see him. It was over one hundred miles with no hotels to stay in; so I packed up the camping gear, and off we were to see him. Pioche is in the higher elevations of Nevada in the Utah State Line. It was a beautiful place, next to Eagle Valley. It's a picturesque Lake surrounded by high mountains, and deer everywhere.

I found us a nice place to set camp. It was off the road, behind some trees, and right next to a stream.

I pitched a tent, and built a fire. It was great. Monica and Gavin had never been camping before. I caught crawdads in the stream. We ate these with a hotdog and hamburger on an open fire. We had a great time telling stories while enjoying the fresh mountain air. The next morning, we got up, packed up our camp, and ate a great open fire cooked breakfast. I put out the fire; while Gail and Monica clean the dishes. Then, we were off to see Rob.

The camp was much better than the prison. We went inside; and he was sitting there with a huge smile on his face. He looked so good and healthy. We all hugged, sat down, and started our visit. We had a great time with him.

On the way home, we stopped at the lake on the side of the highway to have some lunch. We were sitting at a picnic table, eating, when we heard some noise in the bushes. Lo and behold! Out walks a doe and her fawns. They passed us, crossed the road, went into the reeds on the other side, then, they disappeared.

We were about halfway home, out in the middle of nowhere. There were no cars in sight; and it was hot outside. Gail told me that she saw someone up the road; and as we got closer, we all saw a tall, old black man standing on the side of the road, shirtless, in shorts and tennis shoes. He was standing next to a shopping cart, with only a bottle of water.

It was so strange. We all looked at each other. As we passed, I slowed down. I looked the man square in the eyes as I passed. I hit the brakes to stop to see if he needed help. When I looked in my rearview mirror, he was gone; nowhere to be seen. It sent chills up my spine. I know he was there. We all saw him; but he disappeared into thin air. It was the strangest thing. I instantly started praying. I don't know why; I just did.

We made it home safely, late that afternoon. We unpacked the truck, and got some rest. Time passed; and Rob got out of jail in 2010. We resumed our lives. One day, my mom called me and told me my father had died. I was crushed; but could not afford to fly to Georgia for his funeral. Not long after that, my 25 years old niece died. Another year later, Gail's mother died in Hawaii. Dianne, my sister, died in Alaska. Another year later, David, my younger brother, died. It seemed like everyone close to us was dying. My brother, Larry, called me. He said he was driving back to Mom's, and asked if I wanted to go with him. I told him that I would. The next day, Larry came to pick me up.

Chapter 23

Larry picked me up; and off we were to mom's house. We missed David's funeral because he was cremated. He was a very large man, approximately 400 pounds or more.

This was the first time Larry and I had ever spent time alone together. Two thousand miles of talking about old memories, and getting caught up in each other's lives. We had missed so much. I don't think either of us have ever laughed so much.

We drove straight through: sleeping in the car, and munching out. Occasionally, we stopped for a good meal. We made it to Mom's house in two and a half days; both of us tired and weary. Again, she had a feast waiting for us. There was always plenty of food.

There were aunts, uncles, cousins, brothers, and sisters that I had not seen in many, many years. When Larry and I left Las Vegas, we were very limited on money; that's why we snacked and slept in the car on our trip. When we arrived at mom's, my Aunt handed us both $300 a-piece, and gave us a hug. She said that God told her we needed it; we felt so blessed. We thanked her, and gave her a big hug and a kiss in return.

Larry and I had the privilege to stay at the house of our youngest brother, Mark, with his wife and two sons. Mark and I used to be best of friends; but we had only talked on the phone a couple of times in the past fifteen years. I really missed him. It was so good to see him, and my childhood friend, Mark, whom I had not spoken to in twenty years. He came over; and we had a lot to catch up on— only I had nothing to be proud of. They spoke of how God had blessed their lives. I had nothing. I did not want to tell them about my problems. I was so ashamed of how I had lived my life.

Our family recently had a family reunion; neither Larry or I got to attend. When they found out that we were coming, despite short notice, they put together a massive reunion on my 47th birthday. They had a huge birthday cake for me. It was the first birthday party I had. I was blessed. I just wish my wife and sons could have been there. It was the best time I had in many, many years. They made me feel so special that I cried in appreciation. It was truly the best time of my life.

Chapter 24

Larry and I got to stay for only a week; then, we had to return home. We said our goodbyes, and went on our way. We shared driving so we could cover more miles. We drove all the way to Arlington, Texas. That night, it was cold and pouring rain. We could not find a room; so, at a truck stop, we slept in the car.

When we woke up the next morning, the ground and car was covered in snow. We went inside the truck stop for a bathroom break, a bite of breakfast, and some hot coffee. We were standing in the lobby, watching the TV to check out the weather. We could not believe what we were seeing. There was a massive cold front moving down from the north. Everything was frozen, and the roads were closed. We sat inside; it was crowded, but warm. Larry prayed for our trip; and after a couple of hours, we were able to get on the road.

Larry drove for about three hours, which ended up being only a couple miles. We caught up to the snow plows outside of a department store just off the highway. There, we had to pull in, and wait for the plows to clear the road. The store was the only thing open—no other stores, restaurants. Nothing at all. To kill some time, we went inside. I sent Gail some money; and we walked around for a couple of hours until we saw the traffic outside slowly moving. We hit the road. I drove, this time around. I had a little bit more experience driving on ice than Larry did. His Dodge Caravan was great on ice; but that may be because God had the wheel. We could only do about thirty to forty miles per hour; so it took us about six or seven hours to cover two hundred miles to El Paso, Texas, where Larry's daughter and her husband lived.

We rode in the evening; and as always, there was food waiting. She even had a pan of fresh brownies, my favorite. We talked for a while, took showers, and went to sleep.

The next morning, Larry and I got up to find hot cakes, bacon, sausage, and coffee waiting. She is such a good girl. That day, we went to the El Paso Saddle, Blanket and Indian store that Larry had been telling me about. We bought a few things. When we finished our shopping and went outside the store, it was snowing.

It was six degrees outside. I have never been so cold. There was actually white stuff blowing back into Mexico; we thought that was funny.

Just a little drug humor.

We drove around a bit, did some sightseeing, and then we went to this great place for dinner. We went back to the house that afternoon, and went inside to warm up and talk. We were just catching up and watching some movies before going to sleep.

When Larry and I got up the next morning, we had another great breakfast waiting for us. We ate and checked the news for a weather report. Thankfully, the cold front had passed; so we packed up, and got ready to leave.

We left in good weather; before then, I'd forgotten how beautiful the desert smelled and looked after a rainstorm. We drove through southern New Mexico; and only two and a half hours later, we were going into southern Arizona. We decided to stop before sunset to get a room and something to eat. This way, we'd be able to get a good night's sleep, and could have a very early start for the last leg of our trip.

We got up early, and grab some breakfast. Then, we started for Phoenix. From there, we went north towards Flagstaff. Larry told me he wanted to treat me to a place he thought I would love to see. It was Sedona, Arizona. It was magnificent, certainly a treat.

We finally made it to my house in Las Vegas; and I was sad for it to be over. That was one of the best trips of my life, and it got to be with Larry.

Chapter 25

When I got home, it didn't take long before I was in the same old rut and running from God. It was late March 2011, just after I turned 52 that I found myself at, perhaps, my lowest point. My unemployment was barely keeping me and my family alive. I was desperate; so my friend, Larry, and I decided we would take a page from Rob's book. We turned to thievery. We were stealing wire, and selling it for a little extra cash.

That didn't last long before we were in jail for possession of stolen property. For the first time in my life, I had been in jail overnight. Again, I begged God to get me out of this situation— which he did. Afterwards, I ran. It's what I did best.

Larry didn't get off so lucky. He was held back in medical for a whole month. Until we were arrested, I had no idea that he had a heart condition. He never told me; him being stuck, arrested, and getting medical treatment was the only way I found out.

The following year, August 5, 2012, he wanted me to go fishing with him. His wife and brother-in-law had been ragging on him all day. I told him I could not go because I had no money; so he, his wife, and brother-in-law went by themselves. John said, "Let's go fishing anyway, Dad." I agreed. I called Larry on his cell phone so he could tell me where to pick him up. He was not around his wife; he was tired of hearing them whine at him. John and I found Larry; and we went to a long, sandy peninsula that went about one hundred fifty yards out into the lake where I had to back my truck into.

We fished for about two or three hours when it became midnight. John had accidentally thrown a bobber out into the lake. This bobber had a light in it; and Larry wanted it back. He took off his shirt and boots, then went into the lake. He was maybe 30 ft. offshore; and I could tell he was starting to struggle. I knew I couldn't go after him because I float like a rock; so I said to John, who was only sixteen years old, "Go get him."

John didn't hesitate. He leaped into the dark water after our friend. John grabbed him, and swam back to shore where we immediately started CPR. John held his head out of the water while his wife was breathing into his mouth; I was pumping his chest. This was a nightmare happening. Only about a tablespoon of water came up; but there was no response. We did not stop.

We frantically continued; but I knew something else was wrong. It had to be his heart condition. After a minute or so, I yelled for them to call 911 as we continued CPR. I was still pumping his chest;

and it was in that moment, I saw the life leave his eyes. I screamed at him, "Larry, don't you die on me. Don't you die?" But, he was gone. All I could think of was that I never told him about God. I hope that he found God somewhere in the last few moments of his life. I've never felt like I had let down someone so close to me in my life; he was as much of a brother to me as one of my own blood.

At the same time, I was so proud of John. He did not question me, or hesitate. He leaped into action, and did something I could not do. The paramedics arrived, and jumped into the back of my truck, and continued doing their thing; but Larry was dead. The helicopter came and went; but Larry was still.

While we waited for the coroner to arrive, we all stood there looking at Larry's lifeless body in the back of my truck. I said to John, but directed my comment to them, "Be careful what you say to someone. It could be the last thing you get to say." They started crying because their last words to Larry were harsh and hateful; and they did not get the opportunity to apologize.

The coroner arrived around 4:30 a.m., and took Larry's body from my truck. It was the longest four and a half hours of our lives, having to look at my best friend's lifeless body in my truck when I never told him about God. Yet, on the opposite end of my emotions was a touch of pride. John was already a man at sixteen years old, and was one that I was truly proud of.

It was the longest ride home, ever. We called Gail on the phone; and she screamed in disbelief. Just the day before, my grandson, Gavin, had asked Larry if he would come to his birthday party. Larry told him, "Sure, buddy. I'll be there." Now, he was dead.

What did I do? I started running full blast to nowhere.

Chapter 26

In 2013, I went to court on my possession of stolen property charges. The judge gave me a fine, and five years on probation. After seven months of probation, I messed up again, and had two dirty drug tests. This violated my probation. I was detained to the Clark County Detention Center on November 26, 2013, two days before Thanksgiving.

I thought it was the worst time of my life. I had to spend Thanksgiving in jail, without family. I felt so alone, and humiliated. I hated myself for what I did, and what I put my family through. I officially reached the lowest point in my life.

On December 2, 2013 at 10 p.m., we were watching a movie on TV called 'The Bible.' I was glued to the TV like I was the only one in the room. I asked God to come back into my life. I was tired of running, and going nowhere. I was running from the one who had been chasing me, calling out to me, "Stop running. I will help you. I will take care of you."

I got on my knees, and prayed to God, 'Forgive me and be my savior.' This turned out to be the best thing I ever did in my life. I thought to myself, 'Why did I wait so long? This feels amazing.'

I felt so free, and relieved. I could not believe I had waited this long. At that moment, I was not worried about anything, not even a job. I knew in my heart that God was going to take care of me and my family. He will never fail me. He will never forsake me. Now, he was in my heart forever. I did not have to run anymore.

I was still in jail; yet, I had never felt so free.

When I do get out, I have a full-time job serving Him.

Chapter 27

For the days showed me the foot prints of my Savior; and I praise His name above all names.

Today is Thursday; December 4, 2013.

Thank you, God, for all the blessings you have given me. I got my commissary today, and talked to my wife, whom I love and miss so much, and John, my son, the young man I admire to no end. I feel like I have neglected to be the husband and father that I should have been. Since December 2, 2013, when I accepted Christ back into my heart, I vowed to be the husband and father that they can be proud of.

This has been the most difficult time of my life; but it has given me the opportunity to clean up— an opportunity I wouldn't give myself when I was still at home. I have spent the last thirty-seven years of my life running from God, chasing jobs, and the most money I could make. There have been things that happened over the years that should have opened my eyes; but I could not stop running long enough to see or hear what God was telling me. I turned a deaf ear to God; and all he would say to me was "Robin stop running. I will take care of you. I will help you," but I would not listen.

I met two more guys in here. One, who I was booked with, has heard my testimony from day one. A Samoan guy from Alaska, heard me talking. He wanted to hear my testimony; so we sat down together after lockdown, and shared stories for six hours.

An experience that I had not too long ago happened in late September 2013. A friend of mine, whom I have known for twenty years, got me a job in North Dakota. For this, I had to get permission from my probation officer. He told me that would not happen; so I went to my lawyer. Thereafter, we went to see the judge.

When the court date came around, both the probation officer and my lawyer were there. We stood in front of the judge; and my lawyer said that I had the opportunity to go to work in North Dakota. The judge approved. I had an appointment with my probation officer three weeks after the court date; and I decided to see if he would let me ride back during my off weeks.

I went to see my probation officer the day before I was set to leave so I could get my travel pass. He said to me, "Mr. Brown, that's not going to happen."

I went home outraged. After I told Gail, I called my lawyer. He told me to come to his office. He could give me the court transcriptions showed that the court gave me permission to go. I went to his office, and picked up the paperwork. He told me to keep them with me at all times.

I went home, and packed what I needed. It was hard leaving Gail and John for six weeks; but I had to go make some money because my unemployment was running out. With the hours I was promised, I would come home in six weeks with enough money to pay off all my court fines and the bills that I owed.

We left that Friday morning around 8 a.m., and drove to Cedar City, Utah, where he was from. We stopped at a café for lunch. He also wanted to see his girlfriend, who happened to be a waitress there. We ate, then started on our way.

Just before we crossed into Colorado, my probation officer called and told me that I could now pick up my travel pass. We looked at each other and laughed. I told the probation officer, "I'm already gone!" To my surprise, he said to have a good trip and wished me well. I almost fell out of my chair; the man who seemed to be out to get me was wishing me well.

We took turns in driving; it was a good trip. I got to see a new country that I had never seen before. We arrived on Saturday evening, got our rooms that the company had provided for us, and then, went to sleep. I went to the office the next day to do some paperwork, and was supposed to start the night shift. Things started poorly – my first night working was cancelled. I was disappointed, but I would be ready to work Sunday.

On Sunday, I went to work doing a parking lot. We worked for three days. The next day, I sat because they had nothing for me. I was upset again. The day after, I went to work on Highway-804, a road-widening job just outside of Williston, North Dakota. I worked for two days on that job, and sat again.

I had been there for six days, but had under sixty hours of work. I should have had seventy hours. The next day, the union called me from Las Vegas with a job that I had to turn down because it started the very next day. There was no way I could make it. The company that promised me seventy to ninety hours a week let me sit for six more days. Meanwhile, the union called me with another job that I had turned down. So, I decided to go home.

The next day, my buddy bought me a bus ticket for a trip that would leave at 8 p.m. that night. I was furious— the company that promised so many hours let me sit so many days. Now, I had to go home with barely enough money to pay my rent and the loan I got to go up to Williston.

My bus arrived an hour late; and I had already paid $30 for a taxi to get from my hotel to the bus station which was only 5 miles away. Only three other people boarded the bus, but it was packed. We drove about sixty miles and just crossed into Montana when the driver went on the intercom, saying she had to go back to Williston for fuel. We were all outraged. She turned the bus around on a small dirt road and drove back to town, to the truck stop which was right next to the motel I was staying in. $30 on a taxi down the drain. She got fuel; and we were on our way again, two hours behind schedule. We drove into Billings, Montana, around midnight, and had a thirty minutes layover.

We boarded the next bus, and continued on our way. The trip was getting better. There was a lightning storm ahead of us, providing an amazing light show; and we only got a small amount of rain. I slept a little on the bus; and when the bus stopped, we all stretched our legs, and got a bite to eat. Our next stop was Beaumont, Montana. It was cold and windy. We stopped at the small hotel where six or seven people got on, and a few got off. I noticed a girl who boarded by herself. She was about 5' 9", red hair, and appeared to be in her early twenties. She walked by me, and sat somewhere in the back.

Our next stop was in Butte, Montana where we had to change buses again. We arrived thirty minutes late, and missed our transfer to Salt Lake City. We got off the bus, and went inside the depot to ask the attendant when the next available bus would come. He was not helpful at all. He told me the next bus was at 7 p.m., but it was booked. The one after it would come at 7 a.m. the next morning. I was fuming. The redheaded girl standing behind me tapped me on the shoulder and said, "It's going to be okay." I thought to myself, '*What does she know?*' It didn't help that my phone had no service. I couldn't call Gail to let her know what was wrong.

The redhead and two other guys decided that we would rent a car and drive there. We called multiple rental places with no luck. One of the guys decided to hitchhike, leaving the redhead, the other man, and myself. We decided to take a taxi to the airport to try and rent a car. We were there for about two hours; still no luck. Finally, the other man decided to catch a plane for his destination to California; she and I were alone.

Having the girl there to talk to helped ease my frustration and anger. If it wasn't for her, I probably would have ended up in jail. We decided to take a taxi back to the bus depot. On the way, I asked the taxi driver if he could stop so I could purchase a phone; which he did. I wanted to call Gail and let her know what was going on.

At this point, our trip had taken a turn for the better. We went back to the bus depot where another man was on duty. The redhead and I went and told him what was wrong; and he said that he had heard what happened. He took our tickets, giving them back a minute later, telling us we were on the 7 p.m. bus to Salt Lake. He gave us food and water for our inconvenience. He even let me use his phone to set up the new one that I just bought. It's amazing how one person's kindness can make such a difference?

Now, we just had to wait. We met a guy who had also missed his bus to Salt Lake. We started talking to pass the time. She was on her way to Cedar City; he was on his way to Los Angeles; and myself to Las Vegas. We all sat together; and I asked her if she really thought about what she had almost done, renting a car with total strangers, and putting her life in my hands.

So, you can picture what I look like: I am fifty-three years old. I am a somewhat a good-looking man, if I do say so myself. I have long gray hair to the middle of my back, and a grey Fu Man Chu mustache, 170 lbs., and 5 ft. 7 in. tall. She said to me, "You look like a man I could trust." That made my eyes tear up.

The bus arrived around 6 p.m., but we all boarded at around 6:45. We departed right on schedule. As we drove and before it became dark, I again got to enjoy some more of God's beautiful country of southern Montana and Idaho. The bus stopped a few times for us to eat and stretch our legs.

As we were riding down the dark highway late at night, I started thinking about this young woman. I thought about how, while this girl did not know me at all, she was willing to put her life in the hands of a total stranger to drive her a thousand miles to her sister's house in Cedar City. I could not stop thinking about it. I thought I should write her a note to tell her how privileged I felt to be able to meet her, and honored to have her as a friend. She made my trip so much easier by just talking. I wrote the note, and handed it to her over my seat. As she read it, I could hear her crying.

When we arrived in Salt Lake and got off the bus, we had a three hours layover. The bus station was locked down; so we all pick a spot on the floor and went to sleep. We woke up an hour before her sister was to pick her up. As we got off the bus, she tapped me on the shoulder once more and told me that she was honored to have met me; and we parted ways.

This was an experience that I had to share to remind us all that there are still many good people in this world.

Chapter 28

Although my days of incarceration are long, it has given me the opportunity to relive my days in great detail and to observe my many mistakes, and even more, the blessings of my Lord. I have had the opportunity to meet men like me: good men who made some bad decisions, but have asked for God's forgiveness and accepted him in their hearts.

These men have affected me and my life. I feel honored to have met these men; their stories have enriched my life. I hope to meet them on the outside, so I can meet their families about whom they have told me so much. I can also have the opportunity to tell their families of what their sons have done for me; and I want to spread the word through my testimony of what our Lord has done for me.

Today is Saturday December 14.

We are on 24-hour lockdown today; but we have the most compassionate correction officer (CO) that we have had since I have been in jail. He is tough, but fair. He treats us with respect as we do him. Some of the CO's who come on duty must live miserable lives at home. They come on duty with the biggest power trips. It's hard for me to understand how they can treat other men the way they do; I pray for them every day and night.

I sleep most of the day when the others are up. I write my book, read the Bible, and pray at night. Our day starts at 3 a.m., with the medical nurse coming in for the inmates that are on medication. This is followed by morning chow at 3:30. That is when I sleep best, after chow. That usually consists of a slice of bologna, unseasoned potatoes, bread, and sometimes, water.

For our second meal, I usually get woken up by one of the guys tapping on my metal bunk saying, "Georgia, it's 9 o'clock. Chow time." We get up, make our bunks, and wait for the trays to roll in. Chow is usually cold, unseasoned oatmeal, cold potatoes, maybe a roll, and occasionally, a pint of milk. Once a week, we get an orange. We only have twenty minutes to eat.

Every other day, Gail and John visit where we get to video chat; we talk on the phone, and look at each other on a small video screen. That only lasts twenty-five minutes; but it's the best part of my day. When I see my name on the visitor list, I take comfort in knowing that they are here in the same building with me.

Other inmates ask me, "When are you getting out? When do you go to court?"

I reply, "I have put it in God's hands; and I will get out when he wants me out."

They look at me with a puzzled look; they do not understand.

I sleep between meals. Our next meal comes around 4 p.m. It consists of a meat and noodle combination, carrots, green beans, dried out tortilla shells, and water. I pray for my meal and thank God for it, then I scarf it down and go back to my bunk to sleep. I usually wake up around 7 or 8 p.m. to read the Bible. I feed my soul with God's word; and I write down a few chapters in my book. Occasionally, we whisper and talk of southern food, gumbo, barbecue, fried chicken, and other favorites. It will truly make your mouth water.

Eventually, the officer on duty tells us to read, write, or go to sleep. So, I write my book or read the Bible. Reading is difficult because of the dim light; and I don't have my reading glasses. I talk to God before bed. For me, it's the best time. It's quiet, and almost everyone is asleep; I can talk to him without distraction. I think of my family the most, of our good times and bad, and a lot of how I have let them down. I pray, and God reminds me that he and my family forgive me; and I lay and weep.

Chapter 29

Today is Sunday, December 15.

It's another day of sleeping, writing my book, and feeding my soul with the word of God. I'm talking to God more than ever; he has truly set me free.

Tom is gone; and I don't know if he got released or transferred. I watch the faces come and go like a revolving door. It breaks my heart to see the young men that come and go, acting like it's cool being in jail. This is my first time; and certainly, my last. It's surely the most humiliating time of my life. How anyone could think being in here is cool is beyond me. I just pray and wait for the day I hear my bunk name be called out, "Number 39, Brown." I will surely praise God out loud, and rejoice on my way out the door.

Today is Monday, December 16.

I'm up at 3 a.m. for our usual cold, flat oatmeal, roll of something that is cold and resembles a sausage patty, and orange. I traded my sausage for an orange; we are always trading for something. Most the time, if I don't want something, I just give it away.

After breakfast, I read a few more chapters, talked to God, and went to sleep. Lunch came with two pieces of bread, a slice of bologna, cold potatoes, and slaw. It certainly was not KFC slaw, which is my favorite. The best part of lunch is walking by the visitor wall to see if my name is on the list. It was; and I was so happy my wife and son were here to see me at 10 a.m. I scarfed down my food, and looked at the list just to see it again and make sure I wasn't dreaming. I went back to my bunk and prayed, thanking God that Gail and John were in the same building. I had fifteen minutes; so I sat on the edge of my bed with both feet tapping the floor, and watching the clock. It was the longest fifteen minutes. To pass the time, I dropped and did thirty push-ups.

It was time. I got to my booth, picked up the phone receiver; and there was my beautiful wife and son on the screen, but I could not hear them. I had not talked to them in four days; so it was really frustrating. After about ten minutes of my twenty-five, someone told me to hit the receiver, which I did, and it worked. The rest of the visit was good, but I hated to see them go.

After my visit, I went to my bunk and prayed as I usually do, then went to sleep until dinner at 4 p.m. After dinner, I slept a little; but when our free time came around, I read my Bible and prayed. I couldn't get to sleep again, so I watched some television. I was sitting at a table alone, writing a little in my book. A man we called '*Doc*' came over to me. We called him that because he was an Army ranger and combat medic in Iraq. He was around my age. He had short gray hair, a beard, and glasses. He said to me, "Come over and watch TV with an old man." We kid around a lot; we are some of the oldest men in here.

He asked, "What are you writing?" After I told him it was an autobiography of my life, he asked, "Who would want to read about your life?"

I thought for a minute and said, "Two people in here have read it already; and they said it changed their lives— because theirs were much like mine, running from God."

Doc said, "Y'know what, so have I." He began telling me a few stories of his life, and people's lives that he has changed, and lives he could not. He once lost a job because he saved a young man's life while other paramedics stood around waiting for a helicopter. The man is truly amazing.

I met Scott yesterday for the first time. He's a tall man who's as old as I am with long gray hair, and a beard; he looks very similar to my brother, Larry. Scott was in here for growing pot; so we kind of hit it off because much of my life revolved around pot. We both smoked it most of our lives. Word has gotten around that I'm a writer, or writing an autobiography; so some people call me '*The Writer of Georgia.*' I take it as a compliment. I've never written anything in my life; and I didn't pass English in school. Scott came over and asked if he could read what I have been writing. I agreed and handed him the pad. He started reading; so I read my Bible, then went to sleep.

In the morning, Scott told me that he read the entire book in one night, without putting it down. It changed his life; and he could relate to it so much— and that it bought back memories. That really meant a lot to me, and touched my heart. He also told me he might know someone who could publish it. That would be awesome.

Chapter 30

It is now 2 a.m. on Tuesday, December 17.

I had one of the most difficult nights I have had since being incarcerated. I miss my family more than ever. I have not shaved in three weeks; and I look like Willie Nelson. Hence, most of the guys in here call me that.

Last night, I went to the rec yard, worked out a bit, and played some basketball. It was funny because they said, for an old man, I was in pretty good shape. I'm tough too.

Somehow, the CO's lost my commissary sheet; so I got nothing yesterday. No soap, no shampoo, no snacks – nothing. I just got in from the rec yard where I worked out with a Samoan guy named Josh, and a Tongan guy named Jesse. It was pretty cool. They are both in their early twenties; and they could not believe that I did the same workout that they did. I have their respect; and they have mine. Then, I played basketball with a nineteen year old kid named Matt. He seems to be a good kid, but I would much rather be with John right now.

Our CO's tonight are a trainee, and a big woman who looks like she could kick some ass. As long as we stay quiet, it's not too bad; but there are some loudmouths in here that just cannot shut up. Everyone else is watching TV or playing cards. I just sit at my bunk, thinking about my family, reading the Bible, and writing.

I've been up all night, reading; and these beautiful passages have really strong meaning for me. God will never forsake me, or turn his back on me; and he will always love me. I know in my heart that he has forgiven me. He has set me free of my sins. The judges have no power over his Word.

God has already shown me that he will provide for me and my family as long as I put my faith in him. I love and praise His name. My family will walk in his path. If I did not have him in my heart, then I would surely crumble and wither away. Thank you, Lord, for saving my soul.

Today is December 19.

Gail came to see me last night at 7 p.m., and it was so good to see her. She is so beautiful. She was crying when she told me that my friend had told her and John that they had to leave. He also told her to tell me that I was no longer his friend. It hurts; but it did not surprise me. He gave her a bill for $400, and said that is what he owed me over the course of our friendship. He put a monetary value on everything he had done, and gave no consideration for the things that Gail and I have done for him out of love and kindness – or simply because he was my friend.

He is my friend; but never once did he tell Gail to say hi to me. Yesterday, he told her to tell me that I am not his friend. I still love him as a brother. He knows scripture and Mormon teachings better than anyone I've ever known; but he does not have God his heart. He wallows in his own misery because he does the same thing I have done all my life; and that is running from God.

The thing that hurt the most was that he put my wife and son on the street while I'm in jail. I'm incarcerated, but at least I have a roof over my head, a bed to sleep in, and three meals a day. It's awful being stuck in here when I can't provide for my family. The one thing I can do for them is try to get them to come to God. Hopefully, Gail can already see what He is doing for me when she comes to see me. With God's love in her heart, she will feel blessed.

Chapter 31

Today is Friday December 20.

I didn't get visited today. As usual, we had breakfast at 3:30 a.m. I read more scripture all night until 6:30 a.m. when I finally went to sleep. We changed modules on Thursday. They split everyone up into groups of three. Scott and Leroy went to a different module; while Josh and I came next door.

We are on lockdown right now, and that means to either read, write, or sleep. Before breakfast, they turn on all the lights, and make everyone sit up so they can do a count with our faces visible. Then, the CO walks around with a notebook with everybody's card and picture to make sure our faces don't change overnight. They brought in some new clothes that we did not get last night during linen change. Now, I get some new pants. I want my clothes and shoes out of here; the fun is over. After I get my new pants, I'm going back to my 5 x 6 condo to read the Bible until 7 a.m., or until I get sleepy.

After lunch at 9 a.m., we are put on a 24-hour lockdown, they do that every Saturday. The lockdown means that you can't leave your bunk all day except to use the bathroom. I can't even take a shower. Taking a shower doesn't really matter right now because I don't have shampoo or soap. Honestly, having soap won't even help all that much. It's like a piece of leather here; it doesn't lather up at all.

This place is so overcrowded, it's ridiculous. I got two medium shirts; and Josh just gave me two pairs of medium size boxers because they were too small for him. Thank God, because they didn't have any boxers or pants in my size when it was my turn to go up. My pillowcase and sheets look like they're two years old: dull and dingy gray. I don't even have my pillow right now because I had to leave it during the module change. Right now, I'm using two rolled-up towels in a pillowcase. I can't wait to get out of here to be with my family, and sleep next to my beautiful wife. I'm praying that I will be released before Christmas. Thanksgiving was bad enough without them; and I can only imagine how they felt without me, especially with me in jail. I don't wish this on anyone.

I'm so glad that I finally gave my life fully to God; so that when I get out, I can be a good example for John, and the example I should have been for Rob. I pray that John never has to go through what Rob and I have had to go through. John has shown me, from the time he pulled Larry from the waters of Lake Mead up to now, that he is taking care of Gail. He has grown into a fine man. I'm so proud of him. I tear up when I think about it. I just want to get out, and give him and Gail the biggest hug and kiss that I can.

It's 4 a.m. on Saturday, December 21.

I just had what was, by far, the worst meal we have ever had. I was starving all night; and all we got for breakfast was an orange, two soy bean patties, two biscuits, and a half piece of pound cake. Everybody's pissed. I hope lunch is bigger than breakfast because that wasn't even a snack. This place sucks. They can't afford to feed us, or clothe us properly; but they pack us in here like sardines.

It's 8:30 a.m. on Monday, December 23, 2013.

I just took a shower, and watched the news. I can't believe it's two days until Christmas; and I still haven't had a visit from Gail, or John. I really miss them. I know they must be out of money, and would like to come see me.

Josh went to court this morning; he is supposed to be released today. I let him wear my glasses to court. My own court date is set on January 7; but I have been praying that I will get released before then. I have faith in God that I will get to spend Christmas with Gail and John. I don't care if we have fast food, or gifts. My greatest gift would be to spend time with them. I hope they feel the same way; I know they do.

Our breakfast was small yesterday. I said grace and God filled my stomach. I did not go to sleep hungry. This morning, it was much better. We got milk, oatmeal, two biscuits, a potato, and a small spoon of apple jelly. I put that in my oatmeal with my soy bean patties. Those have no taste at all. I have to mix them with anything to get them down. I thank God for all of it.

It's 9 a.m. in a few minutes. Josh's court session is at 10:30 a.m., so I can't read the Bible until he gets back. I found that if I pray and ask God to help me understand what I read, I get a lot more out of it. I can say that he does help me understand. This isn't like when I was younger. It's amazing what faith and prayer can do when you truly believe with your heart. I feel so much better after praying and reading God's word— and a shower.

I've gotten to a point where I can braid my hair. I don't know how it looks, but it feels better. I really would like to go outside. I want to see the blue sky, the mountains, and perhaps, feel a breeze on my face. These are things I have taken for granted. I would even like to see the traffic and people walking on the street.

Since I asked God back into my life, I have forgiven everyone. I honestly have no hard feelings towards anyone. We are all brothers and sisters in Christ. I feel so much better, like a huge weight has been lifted from my heart. I am not worried about anything because I know in my heart that God is going to take care of us. It is an amazing difference God has made. I can't believe I ran from him for so long, even after all he's done. I was blind; but now I see.

Chapter 32

It's now 1:45 a.m. on December 24.

Joshua just got released. I am glad to see him get out, but I will miss his company. God bless him. Now, I have no Bible; but I have faith. Praise God for the word I have read. It has helped me understand so much; and I am so thankful that I will have the Lord, Jesus Christ, to keep me company.

All my friends are gone. Every time I wake up, someone else is gone and new faces are here. I am just so glad I have God in my life. He keeps me company, and my spirits, uplifted. He is my Guiding Light.

It's 4 a.m. We just had the same old same old breakfast. The CO just put up the visitor list. Praise God! Gail is here to see me. I can't wait until 10 a.m., right after lunch. Seeing Gail and John will be the best gift I could get— next to getting out of here, of course. I'm going to try and get some sleep, first. Thank God for my blessings.

I just talked to Gail and John. It was so good to see them. I miss them so much. Gail told me that my old boss in California, Paul, died. He was one of the best people I ever worked for. May God bless and comfort his family. He was truly a good man.

It's officially 12:30 a.m. on Christmas Day.

53 years of Christmases; and I have to spend this one alone. Right now is the loneliest I have ever felt. I have no one to hug, or kiss, or even someone to tell that I love them. I do have God in my heart; and that comforts me greatly.

I have been laying in my bunk all day and night, ever since Gail and John came to see me. Gail said they would come back to see me today; and I can't wait. She told me yesterday that Terrie might come and pick her and John up to take them to her house. I'm so glad. It's been about eight or nine years since Terrie invited Gail to her house.

Breakfast will be around in about two and a half hours. All the other inmates are having noodle soup right now for their Christmas breakfast. They just turned the hot water back on; it's been off all day. We've been on lockdown all day too. I've seen inmates come and go; some with charges more serious than mine. I don't understand, but I know it is God's will that I am still here. I don't understand, but I have faith in him for I know he has a reason. I just don't know what it is yet.

Commissary is tonight. We fill out our orders; but we don't get it in until Thursday. This is a really good thing because I only have four sheets of paper left. I'm going to ask Gail to call Scott, one of the guys who already left this place, tomorrow to see if he could do a fundraiser for us so I can pay my fines and court costs. I wanted so bad to get my felony charge dropped to a gross misdemeanor, and, possibly, my probation dropped. It was also to ask my friend if we can still use his address; I don't know if I have to have a residence to be released.

It's 2:50 a.m. I rested a while, but didn't sleep. I miss having my bible to read. That had helped me fall asleep. Three new guys just came in. One of them looks like he's about nineteen or twenty. So many kids come in here; that it's sad. I just hope and pray that John never sees the inside of this place. It breaks my heart to know that Rob had to see it— prison. I just can't believe that I did not do more to help keep him out of trouble.

I would be so thankful if I could take a long hot shower – with real soap and a shave. I have not had a beard like this since 1989; except now, it's all grey.

We just finished with breakfast. It was actually pretty decent. It was flat oatmeal, eggs mixed with potatoes and biscuits, and milk. It's amazing how saying grace before you eat helps fill the stomach. I just checked the visitor list; and I will see Gail and John at 9:30 a.m. It's five hours away. I will talk to God, and try to get more sleep. Maybe I will play a few games of Solitaire. Jesse, the Tongan kid, left me his playing cards. They are worn out, but they will work.

I woke up just in time at 9:10 a.m. Lunch just rolled in. We got turkey, gravy, potatoes, salad, a whole croissant roll, and an apple fritter. It wasn't bad for jail food; and I think it was the best meal we have ever had here. The CO even let me take it to my bunk so I could visit Gail and John. It was so good to see them again. I just wish I could hold them. Now Christmas is past; and I'm going to start counting down my court day, January 7. It is thirteen days away. The last thirty days have gone by pretty quickly, thank God! The next thirteen days should be a piece of cake.

I hope I get my Bible either today or tomorrow; that really helps time pass. So far, I have read seven books of the Bible, and written thirty-one chapters, or about one hundred ten pages of my book. I did all of this in thirty days. Thirty-five days ago, I would never have believed I could do something like that. Next to God and Gail, jail is the best thing that could have happened to me. It really made me come to terms with my life, and how I was living it. The Lord does work in mysterious ways.

It's 2 p.m. I just watched *The Christmas Story*. It is a great movie. I just filled out my commissary sheet; maybe I will get it this time. The CO we had today was pretty cool. He is an oriental guy. He let me take my lunch tray to my bunk when Gail and John came to visit. Most of them won't even let you take any food to your bunk. They will make you throw it away; it's stupid.

It's December 31, New Year's Eve.

I woke up this morning; and I had a card from my beautiful wife telling me how much she loves and misses me. It had hearts and kisses on it. It made me feel so much better just to know and hold something that she touched and wrote.

I read the bible last night for seven hours. Gail came to see me Monday at 10 a.m., but John couldn't make it. He didn't have the money to pay for parking. He had to stay with the truck at a 7-Eleven. I miss him so much, as I do Gail. She was in tears the whole time. She said it was miserable at her friend's house; I can only imagine. I think it is worse for Gail and John out there than it is for me. I know that God is taking care of them.

I think God is making this a lesson for them, as well as for me. It's to show them to thank God, and appreciate what they have instead of grieving what they don't have. They need to ask God into their hearts; and that they need to live for him— not for the way they want to live. I am the one who failed them; it is my responsibility as the head of my house to lead them in the right direction. This I did not do. I was living for jobs, money, and myself instead of living for God and letting him provide for us. We see where that got us. I just can't wait to get out; I can get us on track for the Lord instead of running. I can only imagine how our lives would have been better if I lived for God when Rob was a child.

Maybe this is how it was meant to be. The way I live my life is my testimony for God; it provides me the purpose and opportunity to write a book which will be able to reach thousands of people and places I may never physically go. I could help so many people. I am sure God will provide a publisher when I get out. The internet has opened up so many possibilities One other pursuit I would like to finally finish is my paintball gun stand. For me to be able to find a manufacturer to produce and market that would be awesome.

Midnight now, happy New Year, 2014.

The CO let us off lockdown to watch the fireworks on TV. I just stood there and cried. It's the first time in thirty-four years that I have not been able to give my wife a kiss, and my family a hug at midnight. I just know that Gail is crying at this very moment for the same reason. I did not make a New Year's resolution. Instead, I made a promise to God and my family that I am living for Him from now on. There's no turning back from anyone or anything anymore. My life truly belongs to God.

Chapter 33

It's Thursday, January 2, 2014.

Our breakfast and lunch seem to be getting less and less. I think I have lost weight. The skin on my arms looks like it's getting more wrinkly and flabby, even though I have been doing exercises. My body is not getting the nutrition it needs. I feel like I have gotten weaker; and my face looks thin. I can only imagine what it would look like if I shave my beard. I would really look like an old man. We get no protein in our meals; but I still thank God for the meals that I do have.

I found out today that I actually go to court January 6; so God willing, I will be out the next day. That is usually how they release people. The day you go to court – they release you sometime after midnight so they can collect the last $120. That is what they get per inmate every day.

We get our commissary today. It's been sitting outside the door for the past two hours, but the COs won't pass it out yet. It's like they get off on tormenting us. We are like a bunch of hungry animals in a cage; our food sitting where we can see it, but can't get to it. This is the most inhumane place I have ever been. I will certainly never return; and I pray that none of my family has to either— not if I can help it anyway.

I had no idea that idea that heroin was as bad as it is in this town. I have seen more eighteen to thirty year old young men that are hooked on that drug; and it's sickening. They tell me that it's so easy to get it out on the street— that it's easier to get than meth. I simply had no idea. I just pray to God that I can get John out of this state before he's subjected to it. I don't believe he would try it; God, I hope not. That would kill me.

There's a guy next to me named Brian. He and I are the same age; but his birthday is on February 1. He's been hooked on heroin for the past seven years. He looks like he's seventy years old; it's sad. He told me that he has emphysema, and has two years to live. I'm trying to get him to ask God into his heart before it's too late. He seems like a good guy. He just got lost along the way. I told him that it only takes a minute to ask God into your heart, that God will forgive him of all of his sins. I told him a little about my life and what God has done for me and my family. That He has taken such a burden off of my heart. I confessed that I have never felt so at peace in my life, and how, now, I have the joy of life back in my heart that I didn't think I would ever get back.

I just can't wait until I get out so I can share the good word of God with Gail and John. We can be the happy family that we were meant to be— that God had meant for us to be. I've always known that God was testing me. I just hope and pray that I passed. I do know that God has never given up on me; he has never forsaken me. He has always loved me, and forgiven me of all my sins.

It's now January 6, 2014. Its 4 a.m.

We just got done with breakfast. I prayed, and it filled me up. As we were eating, the CO called out the court list. My name was on it. I knew it was. I have been up and reading the Bible, getting ready for court. I got all my clean clothes, washed up, braided my hair the best I could. I wish I could shave; but I think I would need a weed whacker now. I guess I will have to wait until I get home. I think I look like Moses. I haven't had a beard since 1989. I have a real mirror to look in. I swear that my hair is turning white, just like my dad's was.

Last night, I started writing out our family tree; and I am blessed with a very large family. I felt so sad when I got to Jennifer because, for the life of me, I can't think of her daughter's name— my favorite niece, yet I don't know her name. I feel ashamed. I made a vow that when I get out today, I am going to get on the phone and find out all of my family's birthdays, and the names of my nieces and nephews and that of their children. I want to know as much about my family as I can. I know very little about dad's family, as far as blood; but there is a lot of Indian on Mom's side.

In addition to reading the Bible, another book that I have found to be valuable to my life is *The Purpose Driven Life* by Rick Warren. What on Earth am I here for? I hope and pray that my book will be added to the Best Seller's List. I think my entire family will be proud of what I have written.

I went to court at 10 a.m. While I was in holding downstairs, I saw a good friend of mine, Paul. He told me that he has also accepted Christ, and it's made a difference in his life as well. But, he is going to prison for his crimes. Anyway, I went to court. They revoked my probation, and sentenced me to six months in prison. I don't know if I will stay here in the county, or go to Indian Springs. I just had a visit with Gail and John; and as I expected, Gail took it hard. I told her and John that they were going to have to get a job to support themselves— that it will also help time pass. The good thing is that after six months I should be done, and be able to leave this place.

Gail, I'm so sorry dear... and also to John. I have missed all the holidays, my birthday, and John's; but I will be out for your birthday. If you need to go to your dad's or sister's, that's okay. I understand. You and John are going to have to learn how to live on your own for a while. I just hope and pray that you love me enough to wait for me. Six months is not that long; look how fast the past fifteen years have gone by. If you and John have God in your heart, everything will be okay. I apologize for the way I started this letter. I intended for it to go in my book. Now it is a letter to you, the beautiful woman I have loved with all of my heart for thirty-five years. I do ask that if you can get any money from your dad or Steve, please put $100 or whatever you can on my books, so I can eat.

It's Tuesday January 7.

I had a rough night last night. I woke up in tears having dreamt of my wife getting in the car with another man, and leaving me standing on the curb. The look on her face was one of fear, like she did not want to leave me, but this man seemed to have some power over her. I realized it was the devil in the driver's seat. I had another dream of her talking to another man on the phone; and this terrified me because I love my wife so much. I know in my heart that she loves me and would never leave me. Satan slips in wherever he can; so I pray. With God's power, I rebuke Satan from my dreams.

Now, I'm heartbroken. I was supposed to have a visit with Gail at 10 a.m. For some reason, she was not there. I know something must have happened to the truck. God is really testing me right now; but I still love him wholeheartedly. All of my faith is with him. I just wanted to tell her how much I love her and John, and that I pray they will wait for me. There's five minutes left; and she's not there yet. It looks like I'm not going to get to see her today. I just hope and pray that I will get a visit before they take me to prison. I'm so down right now. I wanted to see them so badly. I'm not going to give Satan this victory. I will go to my bunk, and pray and read the Bible, and finish my book. I know that Gail is in tears right now because they missed our visit; and John is most likely frustrated— but I know God has a purpose for this. I will just wish I know what it was. I know Gail and John love me, as well as God; so I will endure.

Everyone around me is getting out, or moved. I need God's presence now more than ever; but I want everyone who reads this to know that there is a God. He work in mysterious ways. I know that he will soon make it clear to me what my purpose in life is for.

God bless everyone!

Chapter 34

January 22.

My jail time has come to an end; it's time to move. I got rolled up at 4 a.m., got taken downstairs, and strip-searched. This was far more humiliating than being arrested in the first place. I was placed in a small room with about twenty other inmates all going to High Desert State Prison. We were packed in this room like sardines in a can for about an hour, standing-room-only. Finally, the guard with no sense of humor began to take us out one at a time, and shackled us hand and foot. He stood us in a hallway until we were all chained up. They separated us and took thirteen. We were taken outside, and put in a van with steel grates over the windows. It was the first time I had been outside in forty-seven days. The fresh air was good while it lasted. The van pulled out of the jails at 7:15 a.m. It was so good to see the beautiful mountains despite the absence of sunshine. It was cool with overcast skies.

We started our forty-five minute journey north on Highway-95 to Indian Springs, where the prison is located. It was a long, and cramped trip. All I could think about was, '*I cannot believe I am going to prison.*' I had already accepted the fact weeks before; but now I'm actually on my way. I began to pray, asking God to comfort and to provide for Gail and John. I knew Gail was going to be crushed. We had a visit set up for 10 a.m. at the county jail, but I wasn't there. I did not get to talk to her for a week. I miss her beautiful face so much that it hurts my heart; and her voice, that of an angel, is one I miss so terribly.

We sat in a holding cell for five hours, getting our clothes, shoes, blankets, sheets, and the most worn-out mattress I have ever seen. It was about two inches thick, and shredded on one side. We put our belongings into a fiberglass tub that we had to carry down the hill, about three hundred yards, to the cell block 5-D, cell 42, of *'the fish tank,'* my new home. The whole way down the hill, I prayed and asked God for a good cell mate.

We were pushed into D-Block where the other inmates were yelling all kinds of obscene and vulgar things. I tried to block it out; but it was so loud and impossible. The inmates had their faces stuck to the 5x2 windows. I guess that's why I call it the fish tank. I walked into my cell. The door slammed shut; it was the most chilling sound I have ever heard. Then, there was silence.

I looked up and saw my cellmate. He was a big guy named Mike. He was from Montana. He greeted me by saying, "Welcome to prison." Three words I will never forget. I put my things away, and made my bunk on the top. Then, Mike and I began to talk. I prayed for a Christian man; and that he was. He even had a New Testament Bible that he gave to me. We talked for a while, exchanging life stories about why we were there; then chow came. It was cold, but it was much better food than at Clark County Jail. As we ate, he explained to me how things worked. He then told me that he was rolling out early the next morning to Southern Desert Prison, across the road, otherwise known as *'Twin Lakes Camp.'*

At 3 a.m., the guards called him to go; so I got the bottom bunk. Now, I was alone. Even at 3 a.m., it was so loud from the other inmates. They were screaming, and yelling out of the other side of their doors. I thought a fish tank would be quiet; it sounded like a zoo. I could not believe how loud it was. People were singing, and rapping about gang violence, robbing, killing, drugs— it was insane. I could not sleep. My cell was cold, dirty, and echoed like an empty house.

My cell was 9x12, with a sink and toilet. To me, the worst part was when the new fish came in the next day. My cell was facing the yard with a window, the same as the door. 5 inches wide and 3 feet tall, a bit taller than the door. At 2:30 p.m., the new guys would come through the yard in front of my window. I would pray to God, and ask for him to give me a Christian cellmate, or no cellmate at all. I would rather be alone than be with somebody hard to get along with.

God answered my prayers; and I was alone for six days. Every day, I would look out the window; and I would still be alone. On the seventh day, around 8 p.m., my cell door opened. A guy named Robert walked in. He was forty-one years old— and a Christian. I thanked God for that. Finally! Someone to talk to. Don't get me wrong, the solitude was good. I had a chance to read my Bible quietly, and pray to God, thanking him for the opportunity to get closer to him. But having a Christian cellmate was truly a blessing.

Robert was a quiet guy, much like myself; but we did talk about our lives and our families. He did not talk too much about God; but he believed and prayed. Every chance I got, I would tell him what God has done for me. He was in my cell for almost two weeks. Then, he got reclassified and went to general population. So here I am again— with some more alone time to spend with God; and that is how I looked at it. It was my time to get closer to God. I was on my third time reading the New Testament; yet I still got something new out of it every time I read it. I will pray that God will help me understand, and retain what I read.

I sat in my cell for another six days, watching the fish go by, praying that God would give me another Christian cellmate. I only got to talk to my beautiful wife, Gail, two times in one month; but I wrote to her almost every day with lengthy letters. I'm sure I asked her the same questions many times. I would watch the sunrise from my cell window, read my Bible, and pray. I would tell Gail that the sun rises, and it is beautiful— but I have seen nothing nearly as beautiful as her shining face. I would write things like that to her all the time; and sometimes, frequently in one letter.

She told me in a letter that I was only telling her these things because I was in jail. I thought for a little while, then wrote her back to tell her, "My dear, you know you are absolutely right. I do write to you like that because I am in jail. It took me going to jail to realize what you mean to me." I continued on, "My love, I am so sorry for taking you for granted for so many years. The old saying goes, you don't realize what you have until you don't have it any longer. My love, you have upheld every word of our wedding vows. You have loved me unconditionally, in sickness and in health for richer or for poorer, until death do us part, and then some."

I continued by telling her, "You are my lovely wife, my lover, my soulmate, and my best friend and confidant. I have given you many reasons to leave me. I have not always had a stable home or job, but you had faith in me and stuck by my side. I cannot tell you how many times I have thanked God for you. I pray every day that God will make my time short; then I can get out, and have a second chance to show you how much you mean to me. I promise I will never take you, my family, or God for granted again. I realize that I have been a fool for so long."

Chapter 35

February 19.

I was looking out the window at the new fish. I saw a couple of guys that I was in county with. All of a sudden, my door comes open, and this new guy comes in. His name was William. He was forty-four years old. He came in and put his stuff on the top bunk; then, it was chow time. We ate and talked a bit. He told me that he had been up to Bible College in Lancaster, California. He also told me some of his history of crimes. It made me wonder how someone could graduate Bible College and know so much about the Bible, but not have Christ in his heart. I did not understand; but who am I to judge? The more we talked, the more we had in common; and we actually got along pretty well.

We talked about God a lot. He helped me understand many things in the Bible that I did not before. I began to realize that God gives different people different gifts. Some people are able to read, retain, and recite books. Other people are able to preach, teach, and heal. It made me wonder, where is my place in all of this? William told me that, sometimes, God gives the gift of testimony. I thought to myself, '*I can do that. I don't have any problem telling people what God has done for me.*' He has certainly given me the gift of writing this book; and this is my testimony, and it is not over yet.

William and I became good friends. He is an exceptional artist. He drew me a card for Gail of a 1956 Chevy pickup truck, like in the movie Cars, with a heart extending from the grill that said "I love you." It was great. He told me that with colors, he can draw in 3D; so, we use Kool-Aid and juice packs for candy color.

William has no friends or family to write him, or put money on his books. I come from a large, loving family; I could not imagine having no one in my life to write me. I decided that I would buy him a set of colored pencils so he could draw cards and things for him to sell and make some money to get the things he needed. When we got our commissary sheet, I ordered him the colored pencils and surprised him. He wanted to draw something else for me, so I asked him if he would draw me another card with two old trucks like the first one. This one had a 1956 pickup with a single headlight, and a 1958 Chevy pickup with dual headlights. He drew them like cartoons on a stage with curtains. They kind of looked like Mater from the movie. He also drew a heart protruding from the grills that met in the center of the stage that said,

"Together forever." All of this was drawn in 3D and candy color. It looks so real. I could not believe it. The 56, or the female truck, was in purple, my wife's favorite color. He made the 58 pickup truck in a yellow and orange color. It really looked like two trucks on a stage. I was amazed.

The same day, I got a letter from Gail and John. John was now eighteen years old. He asked me, "How is the fish tank dad? What kind of fish are you? A great white shark?" I thought that was funny.

I asked William if he would draw me one more card; and he replied, "Of course. What do you want me to draw?"

I thought for a minute and said, "How about a great white shark getting ready to eat a small fish, like in the cartoon movie 'Finding Nemo." He agreed, and started on it right away. About three hours later, he handed it to me. I was astounded. It looked so real. I mean everything looked real. The rocks, the sea shells, the sand, and nineteen little signs that said, "Beware of sharks." I was looking into a real aquarium. William is probably the best artist I have ever known.

I told him that I was writing a book of my testimony of what God has done for me. He asked what the title of it was, and I told him that it was called *'The Life of a Running Man.'* I explained to him why I called it that: I've ran from God my whole life. Then, he asked what the cover was going to look like. I had no idea. I couldn't come up with anything that I thought was appropriate. As we were talking, we were looking at a map of the United States that I had drawn lines on, to and from all the states and cities that I have been to across the country— from California, to Florida, Hawaii, Oregon, Montana, North Dakota, Wisconsin, and everywhere in between. William suggested using a picture of a map with a picture of me from everywhere I have been in life. I thought it was a great idea; it's just what I wanted and didn't know it. So, to the cover of my book, I owe to William, one of the greatest men I have ever met.

The next day, I got reclassified. I was moved into general population at High Desert State Prison. I thought it was ironic because both Rob and I helped build it; and we were both going to be prisoners there. Of course, he already served his time. I was told that I would be going to a fire camp in the future.

That afternoon, I was moved into a different unit. I have never seen William since. I got put into a cell with this guy named Baca. He said he was a Christian and had read the Bible; but he still had a hard heart. We talked the first day; but he made me feel uncomfortable, like I was invading his space. I guess he had been in prison for two or three times; and this time, he had been in since September of 2013. When I got settled in, he looked at my mattress and said, "You've been sleeping on this for a month?"

I said, "Yes, only this one." It looked like it was about ten years old, split, and only about two inches thick.

He said, "I have to go to court on Tuesday. When I come back, I will get you a new mattress from intake. I like you. I know the guys up there; and it won't be a problem."

Tuesday came around; and he rolled up all of the stuff— that's just what you have to do. He took my old mattress; and when he got back that afternoon, he had a new mattress for me. I thought that was great. We got along. We didn't talk that much, but he did keep things clean.

I spent most of the next two weeks on my top bunk, 3 feet wide by 7 feet long and 5 feet off the floor. I have never been more uncomfortable in my life. Baca had a TV; but he hardly ever turned it on. I didn't really understand that. I figured a TV would help pass the time. Still, it didn't really matter much to me because I spent most of my time reading the word of God, praying, and writing to my family and beautiful wife.

That was all I really needed. The best part of being in general population was I got to use the phone every day to call Gail; we were able to walk up to the chow hall to eat; and we had an hour and a half a day for yard time. That felt amazing because I have not had sun of my face in three and a half months.

I was in general population for one week; then, there were two fights on the yard. We got locked down for five days. That was like being back in the fish tank. No walk to the chow hall, no phone— it was bad. We finally got off lockdown on a Tuesday. I called Gail immediately to let her know what had happened. I knew she was worried. It was good to hear her beautiful voice. It was only for three minutes before my phone time ran out; and back to the cell I went.

I did not like going out for our tier time other than to use the phone; all the inmates were out there talking and bragging about their crimes, and how many times they have been to prison. They talked about murder, robberies, drugs, and everything in between. No one wanted to hear about God or anything good. All they wanted to do was get out, get right back into what got them in here in the first place. I could not believe it, and, well, that night, on the way to chow, the guard told me I was getting rolled up for camp the next morning.

Chapter 36

Today is Thursday March 13 at 2 a.m.

After doing an inventory of my property, which was not very much, all of my belongings went into a green duffel bag, and was tagged. The guard told me I was going to Stewart Camp, somewhere up by Reno, Nevada. I thought it was great. Now, Gail and John could come see me. It was too far; but what could I do other than pray? That's exactly what I did. I went back to my cell and prayed. Then, I waited for them to call my name. I did not sleep at all.

The guard finally open my cell door. I said goodbye to Baca and pushed my tub with my sheets and mattress down the hall; and I will never forget the sound of that slamming door behind me. Everyone going to camp met out in the yard. I saw Eric, a kid that I met at Clark County. He was one that I prayed with, and helped lead to Christ. He was scared to death of what was to come.

There were about twenty-five to thirty inmates going to a different camp across the state. The guards put us in holding cells, packing us in like sardines. Then, we were given sack lunches. That was our breakfast: more bologna sandwiches and a boiled egg. I ate the egg, and gave the bologna away. I was not hungry at all. After about two hours of just standing there, we had to strip down, one at a time— and I do mean all the way down to our birthday suits. It was totally humiliating. We were searched, dressed, and then, put into another holding cell where we were shackled hand and feet before being placed back in the cell, standing-room-only. It was miserable; the guards treated us like animals going to a cow shoot.

Finally, we were all chained together, and given another sack lunch of another bologna sandwich and an apple. We were then put on what they call the '*Grey Goose*,' a white Greyhound bus with blacked-out windows, except for the top six inches. I had to stand up to see out of it; but at least we could stand up. The bus was finally loaded with about fifteen inmates. I sat by myself in the front, right behind the cage. I could not see out the front, but I could stand up.

The bus finally started moving, but it only went about two hundred yards before we stopped at the entrance gate of the prison where we sat for fifteen minutes. The guards checked the bus for stowaways. I guess they did not find any because the gate finally opened. Now, we were underway. The bus driver and guards had as much of a sense of humor as a rodeo clown being chased down by a raging bull with nowhere to hide. They were not very nice.

We went about a mile-and-a-half to Southern Desert State Prison where two inmates got off, and two more got on. That took another half an hour. When they were done loading and unloading prisoners, we finally went north.

I had started praying from the time I got on the bus. I knew it was going to be a two-day trip to the Stewart camp in Reno. I stood up most of the way so I could see out the window; but I did take a brief nap after I ate a sandwich.

Next thing I knew, we were pulling into Goldfield Nevada, an old mining town where we dropped off two more prisoners at the Esmeralda County Jail. The bus stopped there for another thirty minutes; then we were on the road again. Our next stop was in Tonopah County Jail, about another hour and fifteen minutes ride. I stood for most of that ride because the seats on the bus are hard fiberglass.

The bus finally pulled into the county jail at Tonopah. I thought we might be able to stretch our legs; and I was right. The guards started taking prisoners off the bus for the Tonopah Conservation Camp. They called my name. I thought it was a mistake; but it wasn't. I thought to myself, '*This might not be too bad because Tonopah is only two and a half hours from Las Vegas; it was still close enough for Gail and John to come visit.*' I think there was eight of us that got off. Finally, the shackles came off and we could move. We got our duffel bags, placed them in the back of a pickup truck, and then we all loaded up into a van.

We headed east from Tonopah, on a highway to nowhere, it seemed. We went that way for twenty minutes, then turned North on Highway 356 for about five miles. Then, we turned left on a dirt road for a mile and a half before we arrived at Tonopah Conservation Camp in the middle of nowhere.

We got out of the van, grabbed our bags, and took them inside the property room next to the gym. There was plenty of fresh air and sunshine here. The commanding officer LT greeted us with a warm welcome. He guided us into the gym, and told us once again to strip down to our birthday suits, bend over and cough. That was the second time in six hours. I felt violated. I have never had that many men want to see me naked in one day in my whole life. As he checked my clothes for contraband, he took my glasses and broke them. I've had my glasses taped ever since I was in county, which was three and a half months ago; it took him only five seconds to break them. He told us to get dressed and follow him to the chow hall. There, he gave us our orientation for the camp. He kept looking at me like I was the only one in the room; and he told me I was going to have to cut my hair. I thought, *'No way.'* I looked around; there were guys with hair longer than mine.

I got assigned to A-Wing bunk 2F. As I walked back to my bunk, I realized that the place was very different than High Desert Prison. There were no slamming doors. Instead, there were open cubes, eight bunks to a cube, four bunks on each side of the hall, all open, with guys walking around freely — It was nothing like High Desert at all.

Chapter 37

I walked back to my bunk, and of course, it was a top bunk. I'm supposed to have a lower bunk restriction, but I didn't say anything. I met my bunky, Brant. But everybody calls him '*Cowboy.*' I don't know why everyone calls him that; he doesn't look like any cowboy I had ever seen; and I sure have seen a lot of cowboys in my time. He introduced himself as I did. And as I put my stuff up on the top, there were no questions asked. He seems like a decent guy; he was about my height, a little bit heavier, and bald. He kind of reminded me of my younger brother, David, who had passed away a few years ago; but he was shorter. I tell you what, right off the bat, I could tell this guy was a character— just like David was. Cowboy is thirty-seven years old. He used to ride bulls in rodeos; so I knew he was not all there, you know? It seems like he got thrown on his head too many times. He said he used to be a DJ, just like David did.

We all kind of hit it off right away. We started talking about our lives and history; and before we knew it, we were laughing so hard, our guts hurt. We went to chow soon after. We had a great meal compared to what I had been getting for the past four months. The more we talked, the more we laughed. We got along really well. That is one of the most important things in jail, a good bunky. I was blessed with a great one.

On Tuesday, I went to see the caseworker. She had more bad news than good. I got cleared for MDF, which means I can get out and work, but I have to see the doctor first about my back. The doctor will determine what I can do. Then, she told me that I had a lower bunk restriction, and she was going to have to move me. I told her that it was fine, but she said she had to move me. I thought, *"Great. What kind of bunky will I get now?"*

She gave me a new bunk assignment in C-Wing. That was like moving from a house to a trailer park. I went to my bunk, and got my mattress. Cowboy asked what I was doing. I told him that I had to move because I have a lower bunk restriction. I grabbed my mattress and went down to my new wing. Somebody already moved into my bunk unauthorized. I went back and told Ms. Cox, the caseworker, that someone else was already in that bunk. She was upset. Nobody is supposed to move anywhere unless she moves them.

I thought it was going to be all bad. Now, I was going to have to sleep under someone who is going to be upset with me because he got in trouble.

She told me to go back to my bunk until she got it straightened out; so I went back and told Cowboy what was going on. He said to my surprise that he would just swap bunks with me so he could keep me as a bunky. He said that he likes me, and he didn't want to have to train someone else. He said that it took five days to train me. I laughed; and we talked to Ms. Cox. She approved us to swap bunks. I could not believe he did that for me. Nobody gives up their bottom bunk, especially for a new guy. I guess he liked me as much as I liked him. So, I got to stay.

The bad news Ms. Cox had for me was that my earliest release date was now November 24, 2014. I was shocked; my lawyer lied to me. He told me the day I went to court that I would do six months. Now, I'm going to do a year. I can handle that; but now I would have to break the bad news to Gail. I knew it was going to crush her— just like it did when I told her I was going to prison for six months. It's worst now; it's a year. I would rather slam my head on the door than have to tell her this news.

I had only $3 on my phone account. This meant that I could only talk to her for about ten minutes. I went outside to make the dreaded call. I dialed the number; and John answered the phone. I told him first. I explained what Ms. Cox told me, and then I told him, *"When you hand the phone to Mom, get ready to grab her and hold her.*" I knew she was going to collapse in tears.

I was right as rain. It broke my heart to hear her. It was as if she was the one in jail, and I was a judge handing down the sentence to her. We both cried. She was already having a very tough time with the amount of time that I was serving— then, my time ran out on the phone. It was all I could do to keep from breaking down in front of all these other men. I had to go walk to the track outside, alone, and talk to God to ask him to comfort my wife. That was all I could do. I felt helpless.

Now, I felt alone and deserted. I haven't gotten any mail from anyone in a week and a half. I depended on Gail's letters to get me through the times of loneliness. Those letters, the Bible, and God, and a lot of praying. I love getting letters from her. They smelled like her; and I felt like she was with me when I read them. She hasn't had any money to put on the phone, so I would not be able to talk to her for a couple of days. She has no stamps to write me with. This was going to be a tough couple of days for both of us. At least I had Cowboy, and David, a Peruvian kid who was a part of our prayer group. Gail has no one else but John. Luckily, John has really been there for his mother.

Chapter 38

On May 15, I was released from Tonopah Conservation Camp, two weeks after my oldest brother, Don, passed away. It was a sad time. I really wanted to see him one last time; but I guess that wasn't in the Lord's plan. I was shipped back to Las Vegas, to a halfway house called '*Casa Grande.*' I thought the hard part of my sentence was over; man, was I wrong. I always thought I had a strong faith— but I was about to find out what faith really was. Casa Grande had no locked doors. The gate outside was also open. But the guards were above and beyond rude and heartless.

I was there for three weeks to finish my turning point. I called Gail one afternoon; and she told me my sister, Joanne, was in town from Alabama. I haven't seen her in five years. I had the opportunity to talk to her on the phone. I asked her if she would call the guards, and ask for an emergency visit since she was from out of town; but she was denied. It was disappointing for both of us; so I told her and Gail that we were going out to the yard at 5 p.m. for our Recreation Time. I asked if they would drive by so I could at least see her and tell her I loved her.

A guard over heard me on the phone and went up to the roof and waited for our yard time. When they drove by and waved, the female guard saw them. They took me in and charged me with an unauthorized contact, an offense that could send me back to High Desert Prison, a place I never wanted to see again. This action stopped all my movements. This meant that I could not go out to look for a job, or have any visitation for my family, let alone anyone else.

I began to exercise my faith in God in a way I had never done before. I read my Bible constantly, and prayed just as much. I found out I could trust no man. The more I read and prayed, the more I was able to put all my trust and faith in my Lord and Savior. The few friends I had would always ask me if I was worried about getting sent back to High Desert.

I have read many times in the Bible that it was a sin to worry, so I would tell them no. I wasn't worried because God and I knew that I had done nothing wrong. The Lord tested me for four weeks with this matter hanging over my head. I would be lying if I said I wasn't concerned, but I was not worried. I knew in my heart the Lord was watching over me.

After five weeks went by, the lieutenant called me into his office and told me that the unauthorized contact charge was dropped. I blurted out,

"Praise God!" He looked at me like I was nuts. He then told me that I was able to have job movements and visits. I was so happy. I could actually go out in the world again, but only two days a week. The sad part was that Gail and John still hadn't been approved for visits yet. I haven't seen them in seven months. God, I missed them so much. The Lord did bless me in another way. I found out that my brother and sister-in-law, Larry and Dawn, were approved for visits. They were ministers; and they were going to be there Sunday morning to see me. I was so happy that I could not sit still.

I saw them on Sunday morning at 10 a.m. I was finally able to see some family. We had a great visit. It was the first family contact that I had in about six months; I cherished it. We spent the whole thirty minutes talking, and praying for things to get better. I hated that it had to end.

On Monday morning, I got to go out to look for work for the first time. I went to the union hall first, and then to a couple of other companies to fill out applications. I went back to Casa Grande around 2:30 p.m. It had been a hot day, and I had been walking and riding the bus; so I showered and waited for dinner. At dinner, I was sitting across from my friend, Ray, a guy I went to church with and talked about faith with a lot. He was one of the guys who asked me if I was worried about my previous charges, which, by the grace of God, were dropped. He also almost went back to High Desert because he couldn't find a job in time; but on his last day, he was able to enroll in a computer class that saved him. I would always tell him to have faith.

On Tuesday, I went out again on the job search. It was another hot day at 105 degrees. I had eight miles of walking, and a few short bus rides. I missed my last bus by the airport and had to run and walk three miles to the bus terminal, trying to make it back to Casa Grande by 4:30 p.m. Needless to say, I was thirty minutes late. I even called from bus terminal and told the guards. They said that as long as I called, it was acceptable. That was a lie.

When I arrived, the guard asked why I was late. I told him that I missed the bus, and had to walk to the terminal where the security guard called for me to verify where I was and what time. I told the guard to call the places I went, and the bus terminal; but he just told me it was easier to assume I was lying than to call and verify my truth. So, he wrote me up again. This was the second major right up in two and a half months for something I did not do. This write-up could send me back to the yard; and it suspended my visits and job movements for another six weeks. I couldn't believe it. The past ten months

I did what I was supposed to do— with no write ups. I get to Casa Grande, and, it was a nightmare! It was a true test of my faith and my belief in our gracious Lord answering prayers. God knows he's answered a lot of my prayers in the past year.

What I did not realize at the time was that by exercising my faith and prayer, I was also helping my friend, Ray. I was actually being a good example for someone for the first time in my life. Needless to say, I have prayed more in the past month than I ever have; and I really had to test my faith by truly believing that my prayers are being answered.

The six weeks with no movement came and went. All I did was go to church, workout, read my Bible, and pray. The good thing was that I could be going home in a month. The test of my faith and prayers was not over. Because of the six weeks I lost, I only had two weeks to find a job— which really meant only four days. I read and prayed more than ever; but, best of all, I got my visits back. Praise God! It was one of the things I prayed for the most. I have not seen my beautiful wife and son in eleven months. Now, I get to see them on Sunday.

I woke up Sunday morning, took a shower, and got ready for my visit with Gail and John. Needless to say, I didn't sleep much. We had a great visit. Gail is so beautiful; and John is so tall and handsome. It was sad to see them go. Two hours was not nearly enough.

Monday, I got to go job hunting again— as well as Tuesday. I had no luck that week which meant that meant I had only two more days next week and another visit. That week went so fast; I had five more days before I could get sent back to the yard for having no job. I did not want to do my last two weeks back at High Desert. I prayed and read my Bible constantly. I never lost my faith that God would answer my prayers for a job. The day before I was going to be sent back, the guard called me up to the office. I knew for sure that I was going to be told to pack my things. Instead, he told me to report to a trenching company at 6 a.m. to work. I yelled, "Praise the Lord!" He looked at me like I was nuts. The job only paid $10 per hour; but I didn't care. I got to get out of this place for fourteen hours a day for the next two and a half weeks. All I had to do was eat dinner and sleep here; it was great.

Chapter 39

The next two and a half weeks went so fast; plus I was making a little money too. I was released to go home on November 24, 2014, one year to the day. I could hardly wait to wrap my arms around Gail and John.

They were waiting for me outside the gate. I swear we all almost started crying, having them in my arms once more, and knowing I could finally be with them again. I swear, as long as I live, I will never leave them like that again. I will never forget the feeling of touching my wife for the first time in a year. I knew that things would be different for us.

After they picked me up, we saw my parole officer. I was only going to be on parole for a month-and-a-half. I would be off parole two days before my 55th birthday.

I worked for a trenching company for about seven months after I was released. My boss was a good man. He didn't pay me much; but he kept me and my son, John, busy. My 79 Chevy pickup was on its last leg. I had been praying for it to last until I got something else. John had no faith at all; he kept saying that we were going to be stranded with no transportation.

One day, as the job was winding down, Gail and I went to my boss' house to pick up our paychecks. He gave us the checks. Then, he handed me the title and keys to a 1996 Chevy pickup that he bought at an auction. It was a really nice truck, with a good paint job, tires, and rims. I almost fell on the floor. That was most certainly a prayer answered. I told John about it; and I gave him my 79 pickup— he still didn't believe it was a prayer answered. I told him if he would pray every day, sometimes frequently throughout the day, and read his Bible every day, maybe he would experience blessings like this.

When the job finally came to an end, I prayed for another. I started for another company two days later. I was able to get John hired on as well. We both made $15 per hour, more than we had been making before.

It was now May, 2015. John worked a couple of weeks, and decided that he and his girlfriend, Cheyenne, were going to New Castle, Pennsylvania to live with Rob and Monica. Rob told him that they could both find work. Gail and I were alone for the first time in thirty-six years.

It felt like starting over again, kind of lonely and boring with no kids. I started working with a local construction company; and I was making more than my last job. For some reason, I felt burnt out. It was

June; and the temperature in Las Vegas averaged 105 degrees. I was thankful for my job; but I was miserable, and Gail was too. She wanted to be around our kids and family; now, it was just us, alone. She wanted to go to Pennsylvania so badly; and I just wanted to drive somewhere for a road trip.

I finished the job on June 29. They let me sit for three days. I didn't know exactly when I could go back to work; so Gail and I packed up and left for Pennsylvania. We had a great trip. We took our time, and stopped in Moab, Utah. That place is beautiful with its red rock canyons, and beautiful natural arches. It kind of reminded me of Sedona, Arizona.

We arrived in Grand Junction, Colorado, around 4 p.m. We also had to get a tire changed that blew out in the Utah, Colorado border; and then, we grabbed a bite to eat. We wanted to drive through the mountains before dark because it was so beautiful driving along the Colorado River. It was truly and absolutely breathtaking through Aspen and Vail.

We planned on getting a room in Denver, but, for some reason, there were no vacancies along the freeway. We drove on until 2 a.m. Then, we stopped at a restaurant a few miles from Kansas state line, and slept in the truck for a few hours. It wasn't the most comfortable, but it wasn't too bad. We woke up around 6:30 a.m. We let our dogs go potty, and then ate some breakfast. It was such a drastic change in scenery. The day before was amazing desert and mountains; the next day, it was flat land as far as the eye can see, littered with 100-foot-tall windmills for miles and miles. Driving across West Kansas reminded me of Williston, south Dakota, with its rolling green hills.

We stopped for lunch somewhere in Kansas; and I called a long-time friend. He was now living in Kansas City. I called him to see if he knew a good place for a tire, to replace the spare from the flat in Colorado. He bought a tire for me; and we met at a store next to the Kansas City Chiefs stadium, not a hard place to find. We chatted a while. I paid him for the tire, and went on our way.

We stopped at a motel in Pocahontas, Illinois for the night. It was July 3 when we went in; but there were fireworks going off, so we stopped and watched. We love fireworks. We got a room and some food at the diner. Then, we indulged in some much-needed sleep. We were up by 4:30 a.m. We showered, and went on the road again. It was all new scenery for me; I had never been through the Midwest like the South. I-70 was under construction from Eastern Missouri all the way to Pittsburgh; and I had no idea there were so many toll roads. I sure hope that money goes into all the construction— their roads sure need it.

We finally arrived at Rob's house in New Castle, Pennsylvania around 4 p.m. just in time for dinner and the Fourth of July fireworks. It was sure good to see them. Gavin, my grandson, was getting so big.

We were there for a week and a half. Then, Rob and Monica asked if we wanted to go to Fond du Lac, Wisconsin, to see our granddaughters, and stay for a week. We were all for it; we hadn't seen Haley or Breanna in four years. Our trip continued from Newcastle to Fond du Lac. Now, I got to include Cleveland, Akron, Chicago, and Milwaukee to the list of major cities I've been too. May the Lord bless us with a trip to New York, Seattle, Washington, and Fairbanks?

We had a great time on our trip. I thought the toll roads were bad in the Midwest; but I could not believe it cost $40 in toll fees to drive eight hundred miles. The roads across Illinois were awful; and there wasn't even construction for it.

We arrived at Monica's parents' house around 10:30 p.m. We had a great reunion. The girls were so big. They're beautiful young ladies. We spent most of our time at Lake Winnebago in Fond du Lac. We had been given the keys to their pontoon boat; so that's where we spend most of the week. We were on the water, and having a blast with my kids and grandkids. We are truly blessed. We had a great time. It was good just seeing Rob, Monica, and all the kids together. We left on Saturday morning, and headed back to Rob's house. It was another great trip.

Chapter 40

We were back at Rob's house for a week or so. I still had not found any work yet. The union hall from Vegas called me two times in one week; but I had to turn down the jobs because I could not make it back to Vegas on time. I started getting depressed. I knew winter was not far off; and I did not want to be dependent on Rob and Monica, or welfare. So, I started praying and asking God for guidance. I got an answer to my prayer within three days. On July 31, a friend of mine in Vegas called me and gave me a phone number to a guy that was building a wind farm in Milford, Utah. I called this man; and he hired John and I over the phone for $25 an hour. Praise God. I discussed it with Gail, and she agreed. Now, I needed the money to get there, as well as have enough to get us a room, food, and gas for two weeks— or until we can get a check. I said another prayer, asking God what to do.

The idea came to me to ask Monica's mother to give me a title loan on my truck. It was a long shot; but it was the only shot I had. Monica called her mom, and told her the situation. She agreed to loan me $1,000. Praise God, again. Gail and I discussed how we were going to work this out. We came up with Gail staying with Rob and Monica until John and I could make enough money for her to come out to Milford. It was Friday; and John and I had to be in Milford by 8 a.m. Monday morning.

Gavin's birthday was on August 5. We had an early party for him on the first with a cookout. For a ten-year-old, he is an amazing young man. He didn't want us to go; but he understood why we had to go. We packed the truck, said our goodbyes, then, around 4 p.m., right after a family prayer, hit the road.

I swore while I was in prison that I would get us back on the right path of following God and going to church and praying as a family as soon as I was released; something I had never done before. I felt I needed to be an example for my sons and grandkids. I have to walk the talk. While I was in prison and talking to Gail during my visits, she saw the effects of God's love in my heart. She was beginning to grow her faith too. I could tell during certain visits whether or not she read her Bible. When she did read the Bible, she was in a visibly better mood; and the same thing happened when she prayed. Getting her to go to church wasn't a problem; but getting John to believe was a harder task.

John and I took turns driving all night. At 1 a.m., we were finally in Terre Haute, Indiana, but then, the truck broke down. I thought it was the battery, so I went and bought a new one. We installed it, but the truck would not start. It was now 1:45 a.m. John was walking around the truck, totally disgusted. I was in the driver's seat with my eyes closed. I started to pray again, asking God to please send someone who could help without ripping me off. Just as I had finished, John asked if he should open the hood so people could see that we were broke down. I told him, "Yes, what could it hurt?"

Five minutes later, a man walks out of the store and asks if we needed help. He said that he was a certified mechanic. I asked if he heard me praying, and he said no. He said he just saw the hood up and thought that we might need help. I told him what the car was doing; and he pointed out a couple of things to try. Praise God, his first idea started the truck. The man said his name was Don; and that he would accept no money. I told him, "God bless you and your family." We thanked him, and were on the road again. Lucky for me, it was a relay switch that I had two of.

As we were driving, I asked John if he believed in God now. While I was in jail, he confessed to me, he wasn't sure if he believed in God. That almost crushed me when he said that. I felt like I had failed him as a father because I had never taken him to church. But then he said, "Yes, without a doubt." He needed to see God's work directly for him to believe. We prayed together as we drove through Illinois.

We drove all night, taking turns. It was hot and humid when the sun came up; and I needed to find an auto parts store. I called my friend from Kansas City, and we met at a gas station. He said to me, "You know, I haven't seen you in five years. Now that I live in Kansas City, I have seen you twice in a month and a half." We both thought that was funny and laughed a bit, then he took us to a parts store where we got what we needed. We said goodbye, and then John and I were on the road again. We drove all day and made it to Denver just before the sun went down.

As we looked up at the sky, the clouds cleared a bit. We could see the Rocky Mountains. John said to me, "Dad, we are home." Neither of us really liked Pennsylvania; so I understood that he meant we were back home, out west.

We stopped in Denver for gas, and continued on. We still had a long way to go. It was now Sunday night; and we were supposed to be in Milford for an orientation with the job. We stopped in Valle, Colorado, for something to eat. We had not eaten a good meal since we left Rob's house. We ate my favorite fried chicken; and it was so good. By now, it was raining pretty hard. John was not comfortable with driving in the rain down the mountain, so I drove us to Grand Junction where we got gas again. It rained all the way to Richfield where we gassed up. We were both beat and tired. We drove from Newcastle to Fillmore in twenty-nine hours. We had decided to go to Gail's sister's house in Fillmore for some much-needed sleep. We arrived there around 4 a.m. and overslept an hour.

My brother-in-law had breakfast made; so John and I ate breakfast, then drove to Milford. We were late for orientation, so we took our drug test instead. The boss said we would have to come back on Wednesday for the next orientation. We took the rest of the day looking for a place to stay, but with no luck. The motels in Milford were $500-plus a week, a price we could not afford. So, we drove to Beaver, fifty miles away. But, no luck there either. We decided to drive back to Fillmore to Terrie's so we could decide what to do.

We stopped at the gas station to get gas in Fillmore; and as John went to pay for the gas, I said another prayer, asking God for guidance. As I was sitting there waiting for John, I was thinking to myself that it was amazing how we drove two thousand miles for a job, got it, but now we had nowhere to stay. We didn't even have our tents to sleep in.

God spoke to me and told to me to call my old boss at the construction job in Las Vegas. I made the call, and they asked if I could be on the job at 7 a.m. I said, "Of course." We went to Terrie's, and said goodbye once again. John and I were on the road. We arrived at Cheyenne's house in Vegas around 10 p.m. Her mother said we could stay there for a couple of weeks until I got my first paycheck. I thought it was amazing how the Lord does work in such mysterious ways. We were back in Vegas with a place to stay, and a job!

A month later, I got John a job with me; and Gail was back home. That was when we started going to church every week and praying together regularly. I told John again that there is no denying there is a God; and that he does answer prayers. I lost count of just how many prayers of mine have been answered.

Chapter 41

Later in 2015, my brother, Larry's wife, Dawn, found out she had stage-3 gallbladder cancer. The doctors gave her three months to live. They told her to go home, and get her affairs in order. It was on their 36th anniversary when we found out. Larry and Dawn had a great Native American Ministry; and Larry is the pastor of a church in Apple Valley California. They attended Native American pow-wows all over the country, and ministered everywhere. This news was devastating to them and the whole family.

Gail, John, and I went to see Dawn in the hospital. We also wanted to be with Larry in these difficult times; but we could only stay the weekend. I thank our gracious Lord for allowing us to be there. It was two or three weeks later that Larry called and said that Dawn went to be with her Lord and savior.

I began making preparations for us to go to the funeral. I was off that Friday, so we got to spend three days with Larry. I honestly think this is the most difficult thing Larry has ever gone through. I thank God we could be there for him. He is my brother.

One never knows how much time they have; and there's no promise of tomorrow. We need to live according to God's word. Love him first with all your heart, mind, and strength. Then, love others as you love yourself, do unto others as you would have them do unto you.

Love, trust, and have total faith in our precious Lord and savior.

Before I went to jail, I used to think about how my life would be if I would just quit doing drugs and go to church. Now, two years later, we are now clean from drugs, and we go to church every week. I can honestly say that life without drugs and going to church is amazing. I am truly blessed; and my faith is strong. My family is stronger than ever. Even though we still have our trials, we now know that this is how we grow.

This book is my past; but most of it has opened a new chapter in my life— A life of loving and trusting God.

The end.

Printed in the USA
CPSIA information can be obtained
at www.ICGtesting.com
CBHW021501081024
15567CB00024B/262

9 781962 497862